THE CHILDREN OF GOD/FAMILY OF LOVE

SECTS AND CULTS IN AMERICA:
BIBLIOGRAPHICAL GUIDES
(General editor: J. Gordon Melton)
Vol. 5

GARLAND REFERENCE LIBRARY
OF SOCIAL SCIENCE
Vol. 209

BIBLIOGRAPHIES ON SECTS AND CULTS
IN AMERICA
(General Editor: J. Gordon Melton)

THE CHILDREN OF GOD
/
FAMILY OF LOVE
An Annotated Bibliography

W. Douglas Pritchett

GARLAND PUBLISHING, INC. • NEW YORK & LONDON
1985

Library of Congress Cataloging in Publication Data

Pritchett, W. Douglas, 1952–
The Children of God/Family of love.

(Sects and cults in America. Bibliographical guides;
vol. 5) (Garland reference library of social science;
vol. 209)
Includes index.
1. Children of God (Movement)—Bibliography.
I.   Title.   II. Series: Sects and cults in America.
Bibliographical guides; v. 5.   III. Series: Garland
reference library of social science; v. 209.
Z7845.C45P75   1985   [BV4487.C5]   016.2899   83-48223
ISBN 0-8240-9043-8 (alk. paper)

Cover design by Laurence Walczak

Printed on acid-free, 250-year-life paper
Manufactured in the United States of America

CONTENTS

PREFACE

The scope of this book covers a span of time from the beginning of the Children of God in late 1967 or early 1978 to its latest stage of development as the Family of Love in 1983. The research methods used were primarily library research. Supplemental information, however, was obtained by interviewing members of the group in Northern California during 1981. No items known to the author were excluded from referencing. In other words, the citations were made as inclusive as possible. All references in the possession of the three libraries listed in the Appenndix have been referenced.

The author would like to give special thanks to the staff of the Graduate Theological Union Library. Without their assistance, the research which was necessary for this book could not have been conducted.

In particular, special appreciation goes to Diane Choquette, Librarian for the G.T.U.'s Center for the Study of New Religious Movements, and to Debbie Dunbar, Librarian for the G.T.U. Library.

INTRODUCTION

Although the late 1960s and early 1970s saw the emergence of numerous Jesus People groups, none has gained as much notoriety or caused as much controversy as the Children of God (COG). Although they are the largest of the Jesus People groups, they are also the most criticized (McFadden, 1972:82,87).

In the beginning, the COG was like other Jesus People groups in: background characteristics, hippie demeanor, communal life style, a focus upon street work, and general theological outlook. However, it was unlike other groups in its grim ascetic stance towards the world, proclamations of imminent doom, hard sell witnessing, a fully socialistic communal existence, cutting of family ties, and its rigid requirements of commitment and discipline (Peterson and Mauss, 1973:265). It is these latter characteristics which give it "a stability of organization that far exceeds almost anything else in the Jesus Movement" (Enroth et al., 1972:22).[1]

In this section, six historical stages in the COG's evolution have been identified. While this construction is not presented as inherent or as the only one possible,[2] it does offer a good explanation of how and why the group evolved as it did.

Stage I: Search For a Ministry

The precursor to the COG proper was the traveling ministry of David Brandt Berg and his family. Berg was a minister in the Christian and Missionary Alliance denomination who, rather than pastoring a congregation, chose to travel as an evangelist, even though he was not a very successful one.

When his mother, who had settled in Huntington Beach, California, wrote to tell them of the hippie drop-outs flooding the West Coast, and of the failure of the established denominational facilities to reach them, Berg hurried to Huntington Beach in 1968, believing that he had at last found the ministry he sought (Wallis, 1976:810).

Stage II: Ministry to the Drug Culture

Authority. The COG's beginning was forged when Berg left his denomination, or else was kicked out (Enroth et al., 1972:22), and started a ministry called Teens for Christ out of a coffeehouse. Citing the account of the early Christian Church in Acts, Berg was able to persuade his small but dedicated group to give up their ties to the "system" (Enroth et al., 1972:23), and to be dedicated to the work of the gospel alone (Ellwood, 1973:101).

Despite being "a highly authoritarian boss with a dour personality, ... he was able to instill a fanatic loyalty to him in his close-knit group of followers" (Enroth et al., 1972:23). In part, this was due to his assumption of a paternal role. He became their "Uncle Dave" and they became members of a new "family" (McFadden, 1972:92).

Doctrine. On this basis Berg was able to impart to them his apocalyptic vision of the world (Cohen, 1975:24). From his perspective of Biblical literalism, the world was seen as evil and headed for judgement. Therefore, it was necessary to reject and withdraw from its corrupting influence. Such things as broken family ties and forfeited educational and career opportunities were seen as unavoidable "prices of discipleship" (Enroth et al., 1972:30).

Structure. The group entered into communal living, under Berg's leadership, in order to fulfill the Biblical injunction to hold all things in common (McBeth, 1977:65). A discipleship program was organized with intense Bible studies being an important part. Berg taught the classes himself and his "immediate family were the key leaders" (Hopkins, 1977a:19).

External relations. The group recruited its members from drug addicts and other disenchanted youths of the counterculture. Though their problems were severe, the group was able to help them precisely because their answer was so radical in its "all-or-nothing" challenge (Enroth et al., 1972:53-54) to sell out 100% to God (Spiritual Counterfeits Project, RE-5).

They took to the streets and beaches with food for whoever was in need and with testimonies for those who would listen (McFadden, 1972:88). When they went to "straight" churches, they would do so en masse "full of 'Amens' and 'Praise the Lords'" (Ellwood, 1973:107).

Societal control. As one of the first new religious groups to arise out of the youth counterculture, the COG caught much of society by surprise. In fact, so successful was the group in getting youths off drugs that it gained them a fair amount of favorable media coverage (McBeth, 1977:71). However, although grateful that their children were getting off drugs, many parents had a hard time understanding what was happening. They were often concerned that their children had adopted a new family. Feeling rejected, they were often critical of the group, especially of its religiosity.

Also, contrary to what might have been expected, the established churches were less than receptive toward the COG, or any other Jesus People groups for that matter. While liberal churches were critical of the fundamentalism and pentecostalism which characterized the group, the conservative churches were critical of the lingering motifs of the counter culture such as long hair and beards, hippie attire, etc. In almost all cases, though, the established churches felt threatened and challenged by the radicalism of the COG life style. While a few churches did extend open arms to the group to begin with, when the Children began to preach to them about dropping out of the system, the doors were closed (Hefley, 1977:131). The churches' response to the COG at this point, then, tended to be the informal control of a cold shoulder if not a rebuff (Ellwood, 1973:107).

Run-ins with legal authorities also began during this stage. For example, in 1969 six members of the group were arrested when they refused to desist handing out leaflets on a college campus (Wallis, 1976:811).

Summary. This second stage in the COG's evolution could be characterized as follows: (1) Berg's charisma as a healer was based upon his ability to deal therapeutically with the drug problems and emotional needs of his followers, (2) the group represented what might be called a healing group, and (3) they encountered societal control in the form of disapproval.

Stage III: The COG's Radicalism

Authority. Apparently Berg was quite sensitive to societal control because he subsequently had a vision that the State of California was going to sink into the sea. After pronouncing this judgement, Berg and some 50 followers began a trek eastward that was to last some eight months. Although the group was given the use of a church in Tucson, Arizona, this proved to be only a temporary relocation as they were soon kicked out (Enroth et al., 1972:24). Eventually (1970) they settled on an abandoned ranch outside of Thurber, Texas belonging to evangelist Fred Jordan, a previous employer of Berg's (McBeth, 1977:65).

Berg himself did not live in the colony, instead he withdrew to devote himself to spiritual leadership. The supervision of the everyday affairs was left to his children and lieutenants (McFadden, 1972:107).

Shortly thereafter, another inspirational experience also help to establish his role as a reformer. Although he was married, Berg had been living with his secretary. When word began to get out, he was forced with the choice of either repenting (since adultery was considered a sin in the group), or else sidestepping the issue. He resolved the issue by announcing that God had instructed him to put away his old wife, "the old church," because she had been a hindrance to "the work." In her place, God was giving him a new wife, "the new church" (Hopkins, 1977a:19).

Doctrine. From their wandering experiences, Berg drew a strong parallel between their situation and that of the Old Testament account of the exodus of Israel from Egypt. Inspired by this analogy, Berg took the name "Moses David" (implying his role as a divinely inspired leader), and the Children took new names from the Bible. Coinciding with this, the group itself was renamed the "Children of God," having become "convinced that they had a message to deliver to America ... " (McFadden, 1972:94; McBeth, 1977:65).

During this period, the COG held to a basically fundamentalist theology which stressed personal salvation, baptism in the Holy Spirit, and the literal interpretation of the Bible as God's inspired Word and standard for faith and practice (Streiker, 1978:53-54). What made the COG's theology controversial, though, was the fact that "their already radical notions became more defiantly bizarre" during this period (Enroth et al., 1972:24). Believing that the world was growing away from God, they resolved to live in a state of war with it (Jacob, 1972:22). They thus became opposed to the entire American system— the capitalist economy, the government, the established churches, the nuclear family, etc.

Biblical passages about forsaking the world were used to justify these views (McBeth, 1977:70). To be a member of a church, to attend school, to have a job, or to live with one's family was considered to be spiritual fornication with the "Great Whore of Babylon," that is, the system (Enroth et al., 1972:31). By contrast, they saw themselves alone as faithful to God. All other professing Christians were seen as uncommitted, carnal, and hypocritical (Enroth et al., 1972:30). Even other Jesus People groups were criticized for just seeking "highs' (McFadden, 1972:103).

The Children learned these beliefs very throughly along with the Biblical proof-texting[3] upon which they were based. In fact, "no other group among the Jesus People (had) a system of theology down so pat" (Enroth et al., 1972:35).

Structure. The COG's radical standards for membership were what really set them apart from the established churches as well as other Jesus People groups. Converts were required to turn over all their possessions and money to the community, to forfeit personal opinions, to submit to the elders in all aspects of life (Jacob, 1972:22), to exchange vocations and education for soul-winning efforts, and to cut any bonds (i.e. family ties) which might pull them away from a total imersion in the group's communal life.

Supporting this structure was the dedication of the Children to being revolutionaries. The fear of being called unrevolutionary was thus used by the leadership as an inducement to conformity, even if this involved deviance in the larger society's perspective (Hopkins, 1977a:20, 1977b:41).

New converts went through three months of intensive discipleship. Activities and relationships were so structured that there was little if any privacy, free time, or reading materials (except for the Bible), and eating and sleep habits were similarly regulated. As one scholar has put it,

> The intense training can be compared to boot camp in the military, or to a novitiate in an austere monastic order. It is a strenuous experience designed to mold a new personality in a short period, using every trick of fatigue, strain, loud repetition, and authoritarianism to shatter one psychic structure and substitute for it the values and vocabulary of another (Ellwood, 1973:104-05).

The end result was a disciple or deployable agent for Berg.

After this initial period as a "babe," the new member graduated to the status of younger brother or sister and eventually to that of elder brother or sister. Mastery of verbatum scripture memorization (in the King James version) (Streiker, 1978:53-54) and submission to Jesus, the Bible, and the COG leaders as "the only authority in their lives" were the keys to the advancement process (McFadden, 1972:101). In practice, though, the authority of the disciples' personal relationships with God and the authority of their understanding of scripture were subordinated to the authority of the eldership.

The elders actively demanded such submission with statements like 'If I told you to go blow up a bank, you'd do it, because the Lord is speaking through me' (Enroth, 1972:32). During this stage, the leadership consisted of apostles, elders, and deacons (Ellwood, 1973:105), with Berg's children and their spouses holding the most important positions as inheritors of his charisma (Ellwood, 1973:23-25).

The colony itself was reorganized into units roughly corresponding to the 12 tribes of Israel in name and function (McBeth, 1977:65), and the disciples were assigned to particular tribes and jobs depending upon their talents and the needs of the colony. The only occasions for leaving the colony were for witnessing (Ellwood, 1973:105) and for procuring needed supplies, usually by soliciting donations (McFadden, 1972:85,86).

External relations. After being evicted from the Arizona church property, the group split up into a number of witnessing teams. During this diaspora the Children adopted the practice of affecting the garb of Old Testament prophets, sackcloth worn as clothes and foreheads marked with ashes, when they invaded churches and other public meetings to damn them. Appearing en masse, they would disrupt meetings and activities by beating long staves as they marched to a strategic point from which they would either proclaim the coming doom for America and denounce the unrepentant, or else stand in silent but shocking vigil with placards proclaiming the same (McFadden, 1972:89,94-96; Ellwood, 1973:101; McBeth, 1977:69; Streiker, 1978:62-63). Another bizarre practice which developed was the "smiting" of those who resisted their witnessing. Basically, this involved hitting them on the head with a Bible (the Sword of God) (Enroth et al., 1972:34,42).

To symbolize their rejection of and separation from the established churches they replaced the symbol of the cross (which they considered too tainted and compromised) with that of a yoke, either worn as a large wooden bond around the neck, to symbolize the coming bondage of America, or else as a necklace, to symbolize their (the COG's) slavery to God (McFadden, 1972:94).

Berg's proclamation of a new sexual ethic was at first addressed just to the top leadership but gradually filtered down to the lower members as well. When he interpreted the "all things common" principle as applying even to mates, extramarital relations became common in the higher echelons. The disciples, however, were expected to be chaste, for a year or so, until they got married. Such marriages, though, were not a matter of individual choice, rather the leadership would "witness" that two particular disciples should become married and would then announce this to them. Later, at leadership training seminars, Berg often encouraged the couples to skinny-dip as a group and in time he began to encourage mass love-making sessions (Hopkins, 1977a:20).

Societal control. Due to their hippie appearance and curious (or perhaps bizarre) behavior, run-ins with the police occurred wherever the teams traveled, and they were often escorted out of particular states (McFadden, 1972:96,97). Whereas previously favorable publicity had helped the COG to grow in numbers, after the summer of 1971, negative publicity began to take its toll (Hefley, 1977:138,141; Cohen, 1974:33). The NBC "Chronologue" program, for example, "exposed some of the inner workings of the COG" and put them in an unfavorable light (Hopkins, 1977a:20). From this point on, media coverage would tend to take a suspicious and critical orientation toward the group (Streiker, 1978:54).

The mainline churches, of course, responded to the COG and its way of relating with disdain and rejection (McBeth, 1977:69). Also, other Jesus People groups went to great lengths to disassociate themselves from the excesses of the COG. By 1972 it was considered an enemy by virtually all of the other Jesus People groups (McFadden, 1972:100; Streiker, 1978:54).

While parents at first received the COG as just another group of the Jesus Movement, when their beliefs and practices became better known they were branded as misguided or even as dangerous fanatics (Hefley, 1977:129,142). It was the COG's hostility toward the family, in fact, which provoked the group's first serious challenge. During the summer of 1971 the "Parents Committee to Free Our Sons and Daughters from the Children of God" (FREECOG) organized as a counter-group (McFadden, 1972:102), and there were to be others later as well (McBeth, 1977:70).

Claiming that their children were victims of kidnapping, brainwashing, drug and hypnotic control, and extortion (Enroth et al., 1972:30), these parents reached out to wherever they could find help. The answer for many was Ted Patrick, soon to become the COG's archenemy. Charging that the Children had been "programmed," Patrick, a self-styled "deprogrammer," began to fight fire with fire by rescuing (kidnapping) various Children and unconverting them on behalf of their desperate parents (Streiker, 1978:54-55).

Corresponding with this development, the fears of COG critics were substantiated when some ex-members began to relate horror stories about their COG experiences (Ellwood, 1973:110). Describing Berg as "satanic" and the group as "subversive," they confessed to being "saved from the COG" (Cohen, 1975:33).

There was even a parting of ways between the COG and their sponsor, Fred Jordan. Pressure from FREECOG (Ellwood, 1973:108) and "their deviation from the theology and techniques of the Soul Clinic ... " (Streiker, 1978:56) prompted Jordan, in October of 1971, to evict the COG from the Texas ranch and other property in Los Angeles (McFadden, 1972:84,100; McBeth, 1977:66).

Summary. This third stage in the COG's evolution could be characterized as follows: (1) Berg's charisma as a reformer was based upon his divine inspiration, (2) the group represented what might be called a reform group, and (3) they elicited societal control in the form of rejection.

Stage IV: Hostility Towards the System

Authority. Berg apparently left the U.S. in 1971 and became a less visible leader (Cohen, 1975:27). However, he began to guide the group "as a sort of hidden eminence" (Ellwood, 1973:109) through letters which expressed his views and wishes. Originally called "Moses Letters," they later became "Mo-Letters" for short. They were claimed by Berg to be divinely inspired messages from God and he instructed that they be placed on par with the Bible in the indoctrination of new members and in their devotional studies (Spiritual Counterfeits Project, RE-5). The letters provided: (1) reports of Berg's communication with the spiritual world, (2) an identification with and assimilation of biblical stories into the history of the COG, and (3) practical advice for the colonies (Ellwood, 1973:109).

About this time, Berg adopted the titles of "latter-day" prophet and "end-time" prophet. Instead of being merely an inspired leader, he was now the "one" who was to herald the soon coming world apocalypse (McBeth, 1977:67).

Doctrine. As the COG's theology evolved, it began to take on rather heterodox themes. In their developing eschatology, for example, rejection of American society grew to new extremes. Interpreting the imagery in Revelation of the Great Whore whom God would judge and destroy as referring to America, the group became convinced that the country was in a time of "Great Confusion" and corrupted beyond all hope (McBeth, 1977:67).

Seeing the churches as stale and false, the group's resentment toward them grew. One of Berg's letters of 1972 put it in these terms—"By this time we were so bitter against the churches for their hypocritical do-nothing religion, their multi-million-dollar fancy church buildings that ... we were ready to declare war on the Church system" (McBeth, 1977:70).

Within this corrupt system, the COG saw themselves a "building a new communal society, a new civilization, the Kingdom of God" (McFadden, 1972:103). Further, this contrasting of the condemned forces of darkness with the redeemed force of light (the COG) easily led to an antinomian ethic since they believed that they were not bound by the system's standards or judgement (Ellwood, 1973:111). By justifying their use of the system for their own purposes, Berg reversed many of their previous policies. It was now recommended, for example, that the Children should seek and use government support (i.e. welfare) as much as possible (Ellwood, 1973:109).

Structure. As this stage, the group's structure was transformed by the addition of a new layer of leaders called "shepherds" who were put in charge of local "flocks" and made answerable to the regionally based elders. Their authority was not their own, though, rather it was inherited from Berg (Enroth, et al., 1972:24).

As for the location of the lower members in the structure, an ex-member has cynically described the organizational arrangement in the following terms. "Having a confrontation with Christ isn't the big thing anymore. The key to success in the COG is how effectively a person fits into the Moses David witnessing machine, producing more income and more disciples for King David" (Hopkins, 1977a:21-22).

External relations. "Alleging both an atmosphere of persecution and the immanence of cataclysmic earthquakes ... " (Ellwood, 1973:108), the COG left the Jordan properties and set up headquarters elsewhere. Corresponding with this, they began to spread out more in their proselytizing efforts. By 1972 they had grown to 40 different colonies and some 2,000 disciples across the U.S. (Spiritual Counterfeits Project, RE-5). Also, COG missionaries were soon following Berg's example of emigration from the U.S. and colonies were established in Europe and Latin America as well (Cohen, 1975:27).

In this period, the colonies were highly mobile due to their policy of reaping what converts they could in a particular area and then moving on. This mobility was seen as a survival strategy against persecution, and as their critics pointed out, this made things more difficult for parents trying to locate their children and for officials trying to monitor the group's activities (Dart, 1976).

A shift also took place in their witnessing. According to one ex-member, "the strategy is still evangelism, but the messages are 100 per cent different. It's not so much Jesus Christ any more; it is Moses David. And the methods are different. Before, it was street evangelism. Now it's peddling literature for money" (Hopkins, 1977a:19). Or, in Berg's own words, "our main job is not their witnessing, but my witnessing" (Berg, 1973a). Witnessing thus became 'litnessing' in that the selling of literature became combined with getting the message out (Wallis, 1976:822). The Children also became "notorious for using profane and vulgar language ... ," not only in their colonies but in their witness as well (Hopkins, 1977a:18).

Inspired by Berg's messages, the Children began to pray that all the church buildings in America would burn down and that God would strike their parents dead. While the COG has not been linked with any church arson, some members have on occasion assaulted their parents. Hatred for the churches and their families had thus become the measure of the sincerity of their faith (McBeth, 1977:69-70). The group also took action by countering FREECOG's charges with a $1,100,000 libel and slander suit against four of its leaders (Ellwood, 1973:110).

Societal control. At this point, both the State of New York and the State of California began to investigate the COG on a number of accounts (Sparks, 1977:163). The attorney General of New York, Louis J. Lefkowitz, for example, held an 18-month investigation and issued in 1974 his "Report on the

Activities of the Children of God" which alledged that they were engaged in numerous illegal acts including: kidnapping, brainwashing, imprisonment, virtual enslavement, violence, prostitution, polygamy, incest, sexual abuse and rape, draft dodging, tax evasion, and theft (McBeth, 1977:64,75; Dart, 1976:II-3).

Overseas it also became apparent that other countries would be no more hospitable than the U.S. had been. For example, they often had difficulty getting their visas renewed in some countries (Wallis, 1976:817-18), their scope of operation had been limited through legal means (Bruning et al., 1979:102), Berg had had to flee the summons of judges, and the COG was blaming "unspecified 'enemies' for the death of at least one disciple" (Time, 1977:48). While the COG explained their mobility as due to their unwillingness to be tied down with property (after the ranch episode), it was also clearly the case that this mobility was necessary because of critical neighbors and officials, both at home and abroad (Cohen, 1975:26-27). Societal control was now coming from a variety of directions (Hefley, 1977:141).

Summary. This fourth stage in the COG's evolution could be characterized as follows: (1) Berg's charisma as a prophet was based upon divine revelation, (2) the group represented what has been called a sect, and (3) they stimulated societal control in the form of harrassment.

Stage V: Withdrawal of the COG

Authority. Whereas Berg had previously played the role of a prophet by proclaiming his revelations through the Mo-letters, they now began to present a different image of Berg, that of a deified mortal or demigod.[5] This claim was legitimated by Berg through three principal means: spiritual experiences, assumption of a new name, and Biblical exegesis.

Berg began to claim supernatural powers by virtue of his having been filled with the Holy Spirit from birth (Hefley, 1977:128) and through his encounters with "spirits." Although the Bible forbids communication with "familiar spirits," Abrahim (a supposed Gypsy king), Rasputin, the Pied Piper, Joan of Arc, Oliver Cromwell, Merlin the Magician, William Jennings Bryan, Martin Luther, and others, supposedly entered into his body and spoke messages and revelations through his mouth. In Berg's own words, "It is as though Abrahim my angelic helper comes in and blends with my body.... In other words, I could have the power of the greatest of the magicians of the world to help me if I wanted it, even like Merlin the Magician, King Arthur's court magician" (Hopkins, 1977a:20)! This empowerment of Berg was assumed to carry over to his followers as well. For instance, he instructed them 'You could even rebuke the devil in the name of David and he will flee. No power in the world can stand against the spirit in David' (Spiritual Counterfeits Project, RE-5). Berg also claimed to have frequent sexual relations with "goddesses" (spirits), to have visited hell, and other authority conferring spiritual experiences (Hopkins, 1977a:20).

As this shows, while Berg had previously emphasized his name Moses, he now began to emphasize his name David in order to assume this new and more charismatic role (Spiritual Counterfeits Project, RE-5). The allusion, of course, is to King David of the Old Testament, which served to legitimate the change in Berg's role from one of leading his followers to one of reigning over them (Hopkins, 1977a:20). In making this transition, Berg began to portray himself as "God's Anointed" (Hefley, 1977:128), as "the one the world was waiting for" (Cornerstone, No. 38:9.), and as the David prophesied to fulfill the covenant (Frampton, 1972). By claiming to personally fulfill Old Testament passages like Ezekiel 34 and 37, Hosea 3, and the like, which refer to King David who is to come in the future, Berg equated himself with the Messiah (Hopkins,1977a:20). Then, in the use of Berg's name (David) to rebuke the devil (mentioned above), there is also the allusion to Jesus (since the New Testament attributes such power to His name alone).

Believing that Berg got these revelations directly from God, the Children began to venerate him to the point of idolatry (Hopkins, 1977a:20). Their beliefs and practices thus became more and more based upon Berg's revelations (Hopkins, 1977a:19).

Doctrine. As Berg's charisma was strengthened, so was his control over the group's theology. Proclaiming that the biblical Scriptures were "God's Word for yesterday," Berg supplanted them with "God's Word for today," i.e., his letters (Hopkins, 1977a:18). However, the letters endorsed some practices which were in clear violation of biblical standards: witchcraft, spiritism, astrology, pornography, prostitution, lesbianism, foul language, etc. (Hopkins, 1977a:21). According to one scholar, for example, "the sex theme has dominated 50 percent of COG literature since 1974" (Hopkins, 1977b:41). Customary morality was thus dispensed with "in favor of higher imperatives" (Wallis, 1978:72). The theological doctrines proclaimed in the letters were equally unorthodox. Berg proclaimed that "God is a pimp! He uses his Church all the time to win souls" (Hopkins, 1977b:41). He declared his disbelief in the Trinity (Hopkins, 1978:44), and he taught that there would be universal reconciliation at the end of time (Berg, 1973b).

As Berg's identity and role changed, so did the COG's. The Children began to see themselves as "blessed above all men on earth" whose "love" was to be a "legend" (Cornerstone, No. 38:9). Here as well, the Bible was interpreted to support this image. In particular, it came to be believed that the Children would make up the core of the 144,000 redeemed spoken of in Revelation 7 and 14, that is, the restored Israel (Hopkins, 1977a:20).

Structure. With the flight from the U.S., the COG's entire leadership went underground, presumably as a protective measure (Spiritual Counterfeits Project, RE-5). In 1975 Berg's birthday was taken as the occasion for "The New Revolution" (Sparks, 1977:161). The major change was that the colonies split into smaller units with an expansion of the leadership. Although involving a degree of democratization in procedure, the leadership nevertheless assumed shape as a seven-level (Sparks, 1977:162) "pyramid type of government" which ruled "from the top down" (Hopkins, 1977a:19). While this structure has been generally seen as autocratically run by Berg, there has been some disagreement on this point.[6] Regardless of whether the COG is seen at this stage as being "authoritarian" or "democratic," though, it remains clear that his authority continued to be a powerful influence.

External relations. When the comet Kohouteles (the "Christmas comet") came in 1973 Berg took this as a sign that America would be destroyed by 1975 (Hopkins, 1977a:22). Interpreting this as heralding the great tribulation, most of the COG and virtually all of the leadership left the U.S., primarily for Europe, in an effort to escape the evil forces and persecution. The members who stayed in the U.S. did so in order to do fund raising in major cities. Their pitches, however, were made using front names or even those of respectable organizations (Hefley, 1977:145).

Although the Children had previously been forbidden to hold jobs in the system, in order to raise additional revenue in Europe some members now began to work for COG owned and managed businesses (Bruning et al., 1979:102). Entrance fees were charged at some of their discotheques (Poor Boy Clubs) and they began to market tapes, albums, and items with their slogans on them such as coffee mugs, little gold yokes, and tee shirts (Hopkins, 1977a:19).

As Berg's goals changed, so did the goals and practices of the Children. New liberties were granted to date (even people outside the organization), to attend movies, and to drink in moderation. In the words of an ex-member, "I think Berg is trying to buy acceptance, to gain popularity and more followers" (Hopkins, 1977a:19).

The most notorious aspect of their behavior at this stage, though, was the development of a new approach to evangelism known as "flirty fishing."

Essentially, female members became "bait" used in a "fishers of men" ministry. Religious prostitution thus became "a means of recruiting new disciples and allies" (Wallis, 1978:72). While this form of proselytizing had begun in 1973 for Berg and "a choosen group of associates," it didn't become known to the disciples "until in 1975 a lengthy series of 'Mo Letters' discussed this development in explicit detail" (Wallis, 1978:72). By 1976, the "hookers for Jesus" policy had "become a way of life for the ... disciples" (Hopkins, 1977b:40).

Societal control. Regarding the flight from the U.S., the COG did admit "that America had largely become barren territory as far as conversions were concerned, and that they were facing great persecution and hostility" (Cohen, 1975:28). Overseas, though, they found that they were also subject to investigations and harrassment, which served to further reinforce their migratory and underground patterns (Time, 1977:48).

Societal control over the prostitution and other types of sexual deviance came primarily from the courts through cases involving conservatorships and child custody cases. Testimony on the COG's sexual deviance was typically presented as evidence by plaintiffs seeking rulings in their favor, and against the group (Hopkins, 1977b:40-41).

In July of 1977, a letter was circulated (Cornerstone, No. 38:9), and reported in the press, in which Berg allegedly admitted to having been deceived and to having led the Children astray. For this reason he was purported to have resigned and to have ordered the group's disbandment. While the authorship has remained a mystery, it was evidently pened by opponents in an attempt to discredit Berg and to disrupt the group (Time, 1977:48).

Summary. This fifth stage in the COG's evolution could be characterized as follows: (1) Berg's charisma as a demigod was based upon his deification, (2) the group represented what could be called a cult, and (3) they elicited societal control in the form of persecution.

Stage VI: The Turning Point

As all of the previously mentioned types of societal control intensified, the COG entered a watershed stage. In particular, deamplification of the group's deviance began.

Authority. In a taped detraction, Berg called the resignation letter "nothing but a completely fraudulent and lying forgery.... " Further, he stated that this shows "what slimy stinking depths our enemies do not hesitate to slither to to try to stop us, including criminal acts of kidnaping, involuntary incarceration, mental and physical torture and even murder"(Time, 1977:48)!

Interestingly, though, some time after this Berg began to promulgate some "radical" changes for the COG. Citing the problems of the overly bureaucratic and rigid nature of the group, he resolved to recapture the group's ideal of being a family. Changing the group's name to "The Family of Love," he proposed that his followers should now call him "Dad."

Doctrine. Following Jonestown, Berg became concerned about the possible fallout from public hysteria over the "cults." He resolved to "change the image that cults have now" or at least to disassociate the COG from the Peoples' Temple by presenting a more conventional image to the public (Fenley, 1979:22).

Apparently, it was realized that the consequences of the group's mobilization for constant warfare with society were no longer tolerable. The solution was to loosen up and become somewhat more accommodating while still resisting compromise.

Structure. The entire leadership structure, with the exception of Berg himself, was dissolved. Further, the colonies themselves were broken up to form "homes" which are led by a pair of traveling ministers, who report to a regional headquarters (Hopkins, 1978:44). Renting houses and apartments, they now live as extended nuclear families, with one or two single members attached, and they allow (for the first time) individual ownership and management of property or possessions. These are referred to, though, as "entrustments" to be used for the benefit of the Family.

This development was not totally unexpected, though. It was in a sense predicted before hand by Roy Wallis when he observed that " ... it seems clear that the community itself will be readily eliminated by the leader should it fail adequately to fulfill the demands set by his millennial beliefs" (1976:808).

External relations. In an effort to show that they were not like the Peoples' Temple cult, the Children began to return to the U.S. with instructions "to spread love, to infiltrate the churches, to make people believe they are respectable Christians" (Fenly, 1972:22). From this position they are to reform the churches by interjecting their message, and where possible, to move into positions of power in the church structures. Some have denied any real connection with the COG or have claimed that they are no longer members. Being a part of the "new" group, the Family of Love, they aparently see no falsehood in such statements (Fenly, 1979:22).

Berg "has ordered ... members into newly-formed small groups—'for security, smaller families more difficult to find.' His new strategy calls for door-to-door witnessing, peddling cult literature, organizing home Bible studies, and pushing the 'Worldwide Mail Ministry'" (Hopkins, 1980:40).

Societal control. It is undoubtedly the case that the "false letter" diffused some opposition to the COG, since many apparently believed its authenticity. This effect may have been only temporary, though, as it later became evident that the letter was a hoax.

With the advent of the Jonestown tragedy, societal control of new religious groups, including the COG, received a strong boost of support from the public and the government. The image of "new religious groups" was greatly tarnished and one would expect that the COG would have a harder time recruiting new members as a consequence. As Berg himself admitted, persecution had necessitated the changes in the COG's organization and strategy. He complained that "The system is out to get us, and they are driving us from the streets"(Hopkins, 1980:44).

Summary. This sixth stage in the COG's evolution could be characterized as follows: (1) Berg's charisma as a reformer (father figure) was based upon his inspired reforms (both within the COG and those aimed at the larger society), (2) the group represented what could be called a reform group, and (3) they encountered societal control in the form of rejection.

The Evolution of the COG

The COG's history. At each stage in the group's evolution, Berg's charisma was transformed to a progressively stronger level, as both a reaction to societal control and as an inducement to further deviance on the group's part. Then, when the point was reached where the deviance and the societal control were no longer tolerable, deamplification set in. Having already strengthened his charisma and expanded his control as far as he thought was feasible, Berg could no longer meet the challenge of societal control in his accustomed manner. Therefore, moderating policies were adopted to achieve some accommodation with society. Whether these changes will prove to be substantive or merely cosmetic, though, remains to be seen.

Prospects for the future. From this survey of the COG's history, it can be seen that Roy Wallis' "impression ... that the beliefs, organizational practices, and orientation to the world, of this group have fluctuated considerably over the course of time ... " (1976:809) is an understatement if anything. However, his conclusion that "since change is such an endemic feature of the Children of God, no final conclusions about its direction can be drawn" (1976:809) is probably an overstatement.

As has been shown, if something is known about the charisma of the leader (and thus of the group's deviance and the societal control brought to bear) it should be possible to predict the group's evolutionary course. In the COG's case, this is summed up by the observation of an ex-member that "the thing that holds it (the COG) together is David Berg" (Hopkins, 1977a:22-23). This is because from the beginning, his charisma has been the key to the COG's character and evolutionary course (Spiritual Counterfeits Project, RE-5).

NOTES

* Extensive referencing has been used in this section to allay any fears that the data were forced to fit the analytical scheme.

1 This organizational stability refers to the COG's ability to resocialize and to keep its members, not to any continuity of ideology or structure. As will be shown, the COG has gone through a number of profound transformations during the course of its history.

2 It is interesting to note, though, that these stages also closely correspond to the phases proposed by another sociologist studying the COG. Roy Wallis (1976:824-25) draws the lines between the COG's historical stages at the same points as the author's scheme, even though he uses a different explanatory model, that of " ... a tension between proclaiming the warning of the end of time and evangelism on the one hand, and withdrawal for the preservation of purity on the other."

3 This refers to the practice of "proving" one's point by citing an appropriate Bible verse.

4 Even such things as clothes were considered group property (Enroth et al., 1972:209).

5 Other observers of the COG have referred to Berg as their "some-time god" (Spiritual Counterfeits Project, RE-5).

6 Two researchers, for example, have argued that the COG "has become one of the most 'democratic and unauthoritarian groups to spring out of the now-dispersed Jesus movement'" and that policy decisions, which require a two-thirds majority, proceed upward through the administrative levels. They do recognize, though, that the COG has developed a "fairly well-oiled bureaucracy" and that Berg "still exerts a great deal of influence on the organization ... " (Dart, 1976:3). Another sociologist has pointed out that the COG has exhibited ambiguity in this area due to its "authoritarian tradition" on the one hand and Berg's sporadic efforts, on the other hand, " ... to encourage a less dictatorial and more participatory style of leadership among his subordinates," but tending on the whole to be more rather than less authoritarian" (Wallis, 1976:817).

7 For the sake of continuity, the original name will continue to be used.

REFERENCES

Berg, David Brandt (Moses David)
1973a "Shiners?—Or Shamers!" London or San Juan: The Children of God, 26 June 1973. 8 pp.

Corresponds to item 271.

———.
1973b "Old Bottles." London or San Juan: The Children of God, July 1973. 17 pp.

Corresponds to item 272.

Bruning, Fred, Anthony Collings and Carolyn Paul
1979 "Europe's Rising Cults." Newsweek (May 7) 100, 102.

Cohen, Daniel
1975 The New Believers: Young Religion in America. New York: M. Evans.

Cornerstone
1977 "God Bless You—And: Good-Bye!" Cornerstone, The National Jesus Paper, 6:38. pp. 9-10.

Dart, John
1976 "The Evolution of a 'Jesus Freak' Sect." Los Angeles Times (March 18) II-3.

Ellwood, Robert S., Jr.
1973 One Way: The Jesus Movement and Its Meaning. Englewood Cliffs, NJ: Prentice-Hall.

Enroth, Ronald M., Edward E. Ericson, Jr., and C. Breckinridge Peters
1972 The Jesus People: Old-Time Religion in the Age oı Aquarius. Grand Rapids: William B. Eerdmans.

Fenley, Leigh
1979 "On Losing a Child To a Cult." The Oakland Tribune (June 5) 22.

Frampton, K.P.
1972 "Beware—'The Children of God.'" Bromley, Kent, England: K.P. Frampton. 16 pp.

Hefley, James C.
1977 The Youthnappers. Wheaton, IL: Victor Books.

Hopkins, Joseph M.
    1977a "The Children of God: Disciples of Deception." Christianity Today
    (February 18) 18-23.

------.
    1977b "Baiting the Hook." Christianity Today (December 30) 40-41.

------.
    1978 "Children of God: New Revelations." Christianity Today (February
    24) 44.

------.
    1980 "The Children of God: Fewer and Far Out." Christianity Today
    (January 25) 40-41.

Jacob, Michael
    1972 Pop Goes Jesus: An Investigation of Pop Religion in Britain and
    America. London: Mowbrays.

McBeth, Leon
    1972 Strange New Religions. Nashville: Broadman Press.

McFadden, Michael
    1972 The Jesus Revolution. New York: Harrow Books.

Peterson, D.W. and A.L. Mauss
    1973 "The Cross and the Commune: An Interpretation of the Jesus
    People." Religion in Sociological Perspective. Edited by Charles Y.
    Glock. Belmont, CA: Wadsworth.

Sparks, Jack
    1977 The Mindbenders: A Look at Current Cults. Nashville: Thomas
    Nelson.

Spiritual Counterfeits Project
    ------ "Children of God." (RE-5). Berkeley, CA: Spiritual Counterfeits
    Project.

Streiker, Lowell D.
    1978 The Cults are Coming. Nashville: Parthenon Press.

Time
    1977 "Tracking the Children of God." Time (August 22) 48.

Wallis, Roy
    1976 "Observations on the Children of God." Sociological Review, 24
    (November) 807-29.

------.
    1978 "Recruiting Christian Manpower." Society, 15 (May-June) 72-74.

The Children of God
/
Family of Love

I

THE MO-LETTERS

A. NUMERICAL LISTING

These letters by Berg to his followers were originally called "Moses Letters," but later became "Mo-Letters" for short. Shortly after Berg stepped out of a direct leadership role and went "underground," he started writing the letters to: (1) report his spiritual experiences and revelations, (2) interpret the group's history, present situation and future through biblical stories and themes, (3) give practical advice on how to run the colonies and outreach ministries, (4) attack the "system" and its negative evaluations of the group, and (5) make prophetic pronouncements. They were claimed to be divinely inspired messages from God, and have been used by the Children for devotional studies and for the indoctrination of new members. The letters cover a wide range of topics: religious doctrine, politics, prophesies concerning the end time, sex, economics, etc. They are best known and most notorious, though, for their frequent and explicit sexual references and pictures.

Originally, they were published in three versions: one for elders, shepherds, and leaders of tribes, one for disciples, and one for babes (new members). The first were the strongest in tone and subject matter, while the third type were the most bland. Depending upon the intended audience, the letters have been classified as: GP (General Public); DFO (Disciples and Friends Only); DO (Disciples Only); LTO (Leadership Training Only); LO (Leaders Only); and RFO (Royal Family Only). Originally, they were intended for internal consumption alone, but eventually, all but the most secret were made available to the general public, being given out and sold on the streets, and then sold through the mail.

The letters are numbered from A to over 900. Those through number 900 have been collected and made available to the public in books. Most of the letters were first published without pictures. In the Mo-Letter books, however, most have cartoons and/or pictures inserted, thus lengthening the letters.

These letters, as well as other COG literature, have been published under various pseudonyms: Moses David, Father David, Father Moses David, Dad etc. For the sake of simplicity, all have been cited under the name of Berg.

Berg, David.

1. A-GP "The Old Church and the New Church." London or San Juan: The Children of God, 26 August 1969. 4 pp.

2. B-GP "Mountain Men." London or San Juan: The Children of God, December 1969. 7 pp.

3. C-DO "Colonisation." London or San Juan: The Children of God, February 1970. 17 pp.

4. D-DO "Nehemiah." London or San Juan: The Children of God, 1 March 1970. 3 pp.

5. E-GP "Who Are the Rebels?" London or San Juan: The Children of God, 8 March 1970. 4 pp.

6. F-GP "There Are No Neutrals!" London or Paris: The Children of God, 22 March 1970. 4 pp.

7. G-GP Maria. "Letter to a Loved One." London or San Juan: The Children of God, May 1970. 6 pp.

8. H-GP "War-Boom-Bust Economy." London or San Juan: The Children of God, Summer 1970. 2 pp.

9. I-GP "Reformation or Revolution?" London or San Juan: The Children of God, 19 June 1970. 3 pp.

10. J-DO "Not a Sermon, but a Sample!" London or San Juan: The Children of God, 3 July 1970. 10 pp.

11. K-LTA "Casting out Demons." London or San Juan: The Children of God, 15, July 1970. 3 pp.

12. L-DFO "The Rise of the Reactionary Right." London or Paris: The Children of God, August 1970. 3 pp.

13. M-GP "Faith and Healing." London or San Juan: The Children of God, August 1970. 13 pp.

14. N-GP "Scriptural, Revolutionary Love-Making." London or San Juan: The Children of God, August 1969. 3 pp.

15. O-GP "Burn Free." London or San Juan: The Children of God, 14 February 1970. 2 pp.

16. P-GP "Love-Making in the Spirit." London or San Juan: The Children of God, July 1971. 2 pp.

17. Q-GP "Scriptures on Marriage, Divorce and Remarriage." London or San Juan: the Children of God, January 1969. 2 pp.

18. R-LTA "Last Ranch Prophecy." London or Paris: The Children of God, 13 August 1970. 1 p.

19. S-GP "The Revolutionary Rules." London or San Juan: The Children of God, March 1972. 4 pp.

20. 1-DFO "God's Little Miracles!—Part I." London or San Juan: The Children of God, 10 October 1970. 16 pp.

21. 2-DO "God's Little Miracles—Part II." Rome: The Children of God, 19 October 1970. 13 pp.

22. 3-GP "Diamonds of Dust." London or San Juan: The Children of God, 20 October 1970. 3 pp.

23. 4-DFO "For God's Sake, Follow God!" London or San Juan: The Children of God, 22 October 1970. 22 pp.

    Corresponds to item 295.

24. 5-LTA "Boat Trip and Hannah." London or San Juan: The Children of God, 11 November 1970. 11 pp.

25. 6-GP "All Things Change, but Jesus Never!" London or San Juan: The Children of God, 25 October 1970. 2 pp.

26. 7-GP "Are You a Sight-Seer ... or a Seer-Sighter?" London or San Juan: The Children of God, 17 November 1970. 3 pp.

27. 8-LTA "He Is Not a Jew Prophecy." London or San Juan: The Children of God, 24 October 1970. 1 p.

28. 9-GP "The Temple Prophecy." London or Paris: The Children of God, 15 November 1970. 5 pp.

29. 10-GP "One Man-One Vote." London or San Juan: The Children of God, 19 November 1970. 3 pp.

30. 11-GP "Squeeze!—Don't Jerk!" London or San Juan: The Children of God, 19 November 1970. 3 pp.

31. 12-GP "Rasputin—Hero?—Or Heel?" London or San Juan: The Children of God, 21 November 1970. 4 pp.

32. 13-LTA "Dreams of England." London or San Juan: The Children of God, 23 November 1970. 8 pp.

33. 14-LTA "Description of Slides." London or San Juan: The Children of God, 25 November 1970. 13 pp.

34. 15-DO "Four Dreams of New Colonies." London or San Juan: The Children of God, 24 November 1970. 3 pp.

35. 16-U n.t., n.p., n.d.

36. 17-U "Tape IV." n.p., 29 November 1970.

37. 18-DO "Baby the Babies!" London or San Juan: The Children of God, 6 December 1970. 1 p.

38. 19-LTA "Prophecies of the Handmaiden of the Lord." London or San Juan: The Children of God, 4 December 1970. 4 pp.

39. 20-DFO "Let's Talk About Jesus!" London or Paris: The Children of God, 5 December 1970. 4 pp.

40. 21-DO "Mountain Island Villa Dream." London or San Juan: The Children of God, 6 December 1970. 2 pp.

41. 22-LTA Maria. "Letter to the Office Teams." London or San Juan: The Children of God, 9 December 1970. 4 pp.

42. 23-DO "Quality or Quantity?" London or San Juan: The Children of God, 12 December 1970. 7 pp.

43. 24-LTA "General Epistle to Leaders." London or San Juan: The Children of God, 13 December 1970. 8 pp.

44. 25-GP "Love Never Fails." London or San Juan: The Children of God, 13 December 1970. 3 pp.

45. 26-DO "Pointers for Leaders." London or San Juan: The Children of God, 13 December 1970. 2 pp.

46. 27-DO "Use It!" London or San Juan: The Children of God, 15 December 1970. 6 pp.

47. 28-DO "'I Gotta Split'—Part I." London or San Juan: The Children of God, 22 December 1970. 5 pp.

48. 29-GP "'I Gotta Split!'—II." London or San Juan: The Children of God, 27 December 1970. 7 pp.

49. 30-U n.t. n.p., n.d.

50. 31-GP "So You Want to Be a Leader?" London or San Juan: The Children of God, 30 December 1970. 9 pp.

51. 32-GP "Sock It to Me!—That's the Spirit!" London or Paris: The Children of God, 31 December 1970. 4 pp.

52. 33-GP "Dumps!" London or San Juan: The Children of God, 3 January 1971. 10 pp.

53. 34-GP "Dropouts IV!" London or San Juan: The Children of God, 3 January 1971. 5 pp.

54. 35-GP "Did God Make a Mistake?" London or San Juan: The Children of God, 2 January 1971. 14 pp.

55. 36-LTA "George." London or San Juan: The Children of God, 10 January 1971. 6 pp.

56. 37-LTO "Brother Saul." London or San Juan: The Children of God, 13 January 1971. 5 pp.

57. 38-LTO "Correction of Leadership." London or San Juan: The Children of God, 11 January 1971. 7 pp.

58. 39-LTA "Epistle to a Leader." London or San Juan: The Children of God, 16 January 1971. 7 pp.

59. 40-U n.t. n.p., n.d.

60. 41-U n.t. n.p., n.d.

61. 42-GP "'Dropouts'—Part I." London or San Juan: The Children of God, 16 January 1971. 5 pp.

62. 43-U "Tape V (Afif)." n.p., 16 January 1971.

63. 44-U n.t. n.p., n.d.

64. 45-GP "Flesh or Spirit?" London or San Juan: The Children of God, 2 February 1971. 6 pp.

65. 46-GP "The Promised Land?" London or San Juan: The Children of God, 4 February 1971. 5 pp.

66. 47-LTA "Epistles to Pastors." London or San Juan: The Children of God, 7 February 1971. 14 pp.

67. 48-LTA "Second Epistle to Pastors." London or San Juan: The Children of God, 9 February 1971. 13 pp.

68. 49-LTA "Third Epistle to Pastors." London or San Juan: The Children of God, 14 February 1971. 18 pp.

69. 50-LTA "Good Sample." London or San Juan: The Children of God, 22 February 1971. 14 pp.

70. 50A-LTA "Greeting!" London or San Juan: The Children of God, 23 February 1971. 5 pp.

71. 51-DO "Letters—Part I." London or San Juan: The Children of God, 24 February 1971. 21 pp.

72. 51A-LTA "Ministry of the Mail." London or Paris: The Children of God, 24 February, 1971.

73. 52-LTA "Letters—Part II." London or San Juan: The Children of God, 27 February 1971. 14 pp.

74. 53-LTA "Letters—Part III." London or San Juan: The Children of God, 3 March 1971. 5 pp.

75. 54-LTA "Organization I." London or San Juan: The Children of God, 5 March 1971. 13 pp.

76. 55-LTA "Letters—Part IV." London or San Juan: The Children of God, 6 March 1971. 22 pp.

77. 56-DO "Organization II." London or San Juan: The Children of God, 12 March 1971. 5 pp.

78. 57-GP "Flatlanders." London or San Juan: The Children of God, 13 March 1971. 5 pp.

79. 58-LTA "London." London or San Juan: The Children of God, 14 March 1971. 13 pp.

80. 59-LTA "New Colonies." London or San Juan: The Children of God, 18 March 1971. 17 pp.

81. 60-LTA "New Colonies II." London or San Juan: The Children of God, 23 March 1971. 20 pp.

82. 61-DO "The Gypsies." London or San Juan: The Children of God, 1 April 1971. 7 pp.

83. 62-DO "New Teams." London or San Juan: The Children of God, 1 April 1971. 7 pp.

84. 63-DO "Mountain Island Villa Found!" London or San Juan: The Children of God, 19 April 1971. 10 pp.

85. 64-DO "Personal Answers I." London or San Juan: The Children of God, 21 April 1971. 7 pp.

86. 65-GP "Cromwell." London or Paris: The Children of God, 22 April 1971. 4 pp.

87. 66-LTA "Breakdown." London or Paris: The Children of God, 23 April 1971. 11 pp.

88. 67-LTA "Personal Answers II." London or Paris: The Children of God, 24 April 1971. 22 pp.

89. 68-LTA "Personal Answers III." London or San Juan: The Children of God, 28 April 1971. 8 pp.

90. 69-GP "God's Explosions I." London or San Juan: The Children of God, 2 May 1971. 7 pp.

91. 69A-DO "God's Explosions II." London or Paris: The Children of God, 2 May 1971. 7 pp.

92. 70-DO "Stand in the Gap!" London or San Juan: The Children of God, 6 May 1971. 7 pp.

93. 71-LTA "Judas." London or San Juan: The Children of God, March 1971. 6 pp.

94. 72-GP "A Heavenly Visitor." London or San Juan: The Children of God, 10 May 1971. 2 pp.

95. 73-GP "Faith." Paris or London: the Children of God, 20 May 1971. 5 pp.

96. 73A-GP "He Stands in the Gap!" London or Paris: The Children of God, 20 May 1971. 6 pp.

97. 74-GP "Stop—Look—Listen!" London or Paris: The Children of God, May 1971. 10 pp.

98. 75-GP "Prayer for Love and Mercy!" London or San Juan: the Children of God, 31 May 1971. 7 pp.

99. 75A-GP "Space City." London or San Juan: The Children of God, June 1971. 12 pp.

100. 76-LTA "Dear Rahel." London or Paris: The Children of God, 6 June 1971. 17 pp.

101. 77-GP "David." London or Paris: The Children of God, 20 June 1971. 7 pp.

102. 78-GP "The Key of David." London or Paris: The Children of God, 20 June 1971. 8 pp.

103. 79-GP "The Call of David." London or Paris: The Children of God, June 1971. 2 pp.

104. 80-DO "The Ultimate Trip." London or San Juan: The Children of God, July 1971. 4 pp.

105. 81-DO "Prayer of Intercession." London or Paris: The Children of God, July 1971. 4 pp.

106. 82-GP "Prophecy of Deliverance." London or San Juan: The Children of God, July 1971. 4 pp.

107. 83-GP "Psalm 68." London or Paris: The Children of God, 8 July 1971. 2 pp.

108. 84-GP "My Love Is a Legend." London or San Juan: The Children of God, July 1971. 2 pp.

109. 85-GP "Sounds in the Night." London or San Juan: The Children of God, June 1971. 4 pp.

110. 86-DO "One Way!" London or San Juan: The Children of God, January 1971. 6 pp.

111. 87-GP "Feet of Faith." London or San Juan: The Children of God, August 1971. 3 pp.

112. 88-DLT "Personal Notes." London or San Juan: The Children of God, August 1971. 9 pp.

113. 89-GP Davis, Bob. "Prophecy in Laurentide." London or San Juan: The Children of God, August 1969. 1 p.

114. 90-GP Shadrack. "Prophecy." London or Paris: The Children of God, 4 August 1971. 1 p.

115. 91-LT "Advice on 10:36ers." London or San Juan: The Children of God, August 1971. 2 pp.

116. 92-DFO "Inspired and Uninspired Songs!" London or San Juan: The Children of God, 31 July 1974. 5 pp.

Duplicated in item 365.

117. 93-LTA "Heavenly Conversation." London or Paris: The Children of God, August 1971. 3 pp.

118. 94-LTA "The Kingdom Prophecies." London or San Juan: The Children of God, 20 August 1971. 4 pp.

119. 95-GP "MO Song Tapes I and II." n.p., 1 September 1971.

120. 96-DO "Bible Study." London or San Juan: The Children of God, September 1971. 3 pp.

121. 97-LTA "After the Louisiana Festival of Life." London or San Juan, 18 June 1971. 2 pp.

122. 98-DO "Morning Prayer." London or San Juan: The Children of God, June 1971. 1 p.

123. 99-DO "The Shepherd's Crook." London or San Juan: The Children of God, September 1971. 3 pp.

124. 100-DO "To All My Children—With Love!" London or San Juan: The Children of God, September 1971. 3 pp.

125. 101-LTA "To Europe with Love!" London or San Juan: The Children of God, September 1971. 7 pp.

126. 102-DO "The Pied Piper Prophecy." London or San Juan: The Children of God, 7 September 1971. 5 pp.

127. 103-DO "The Dollar." London or San Juan: The Children of God, September 1971. 6 pp.

128. 104-LTA "Pictures." London or San Juan: The Children of God, September 1971. 16 pp.

129. 105-GP "Who Are the Racists?" London or San Juan: The Children of God, September 1971. 4 pp.

130. 106-LTA "Schedules." London or San Juan: The Children of God, September 1971. 12 pp.

131. 107-LTA "Personal Replies." London or San Juan: The Children of God, September 1971. 20 pp.

132. 108-GP "Nitler." London or Paris: The Children of God, August 1971. 9 pp.

133. 109-LTA "To the Northwest Brethren--And Sisters!" London or San Juan: the Children of God, September 1971. 7 pp.

134. 110-LTA "Dear Deb and Jeth." London or San Juan: The Children of God, 27 September 1971. 7 pp.

135. 111-LTA "Questions and Answers." London or San Juan: The Children of God, 15 September 1971. 7 pp.

136. 112-LTA "General Letter on Various Business." London or San Juan: The Children of God, 1 October 1971. 15 pp.

137. 113-GP "A Shepherd--Time Story." London or San Juan: The Children of God, 10 February 1971. 5 pp.

138. 114-GP "Beauty for Ashes." London or San Juan: The Children of God, 10 October 1971. 1 p.

139. 115-LTA "Saul and Michael." London or San Juan: The Children of God, 2 October 1971. 5 pp.

140. 116-DO "Thoughts and Prophecies." London or San Juan: The Children of God, July 1971. 3 pp.

141. 117-GP "More Prophecies on Old and New Church." London or San Juan: the Children of God, August 1969. 2 pp.

142. 117A-LT "Coming Division." London or San Juan: The Children of God, October 1971. 7 pp.

143. 118-LTA "Problems." London or San Juan: The Children of God, 15 October 1971. 6 pp.

144. 119-DO "Duggar Academy." London or San Juan: The Children of God, 10 October 1971. 3 pp.

145. 120-GP "Mountainslide." London or Paris: The Children of God, 21 October 1971. 5 pp.

146. 121-LTA "The Draft." London or San Juan: The Children of God, 15 October 1971. 7 pp.

147. 122-GP "Decentralisation." London or San Juan: The Children of God, 23 October 1971. 9 pp.

148. 123-LT "Get It Together!" London or Paris: The Children of God, October 1971. 6 pp.

149. 124-LTA "Suggestions!" London or San Juan: The Children of God, 1 November 1971. 3 pp.

150. 125-GP "Persecution." London or Paris: The Children of God, 1 November 1971. 9 pp.

151. 125A-DO "How to Close Up a Colony." London or San Juan: The Children of God, 1 November 1971. 2 pp.

152. 126-LTA "Looking Unto Jesus!" London or San Juan: The Children of God, 12 November 1971. 6 pp.

153. 127-LT "Specifics." London or San Juan: The Children of God, November 1971. 9 pp.

154. 128-LTA "They Can't Stop Our Rain!" London or San Juan: The Children of God, 19 November 1971. 8 pp.

155. 129-LTA "Details." London or San Juan: The Children of God, 16 November 1971. 15 pp.

156. 130-LTA "Communications." London or Paris: The Children of God, August 1971. 5 pp.

157. 140-LTA "Backsliders." London or San Juan: The Children of God, November 1971. 8 pp.

158. 141-LTA "Statistics." London or San Juan: The Children of God, 23 November 1971. 5 pp.

159. 142-LTA "Public Relations." London or San Juan: The Children of God, 24 November 1971. 21 pp.

160. 143-LTO "Personal Visits Part I—Sin in the Camp." London or San Juan: The Children of God, December 1971. 11 pp.

161. 143A-LTA "Personal Visits Parts II & III—Contend for the Faith! & What's in a Name?" London or Paris: The Children of God, 2 December 1971. 20 pp.

162. 144-DFO "Let My People Go!" London or San Juan: The Children of God, 6 December 1971. 6 pp.

163. 144A-LTA "Emergency Call Home." London or San Juan: The Children of God, 21 November 1971. 2 pp.

164. 145-LTA "The Homegoing." London or San Juan: The Children of God, 13 December 1971. 5 pp.

165. 146-GP "The Little Book." London or San Juan: The Children of God, 13 December 1971. 4 pp.

166. 147-LTA "Personal Words." London or San Juan: The Children of God, 13 December 1971. 22 pp.

167. 148-GP "Jesus People?—Or Revolution!" London or San Juan: The Children of God, June 1971. 7 pp.

168. 149-GP "Current Events." London or Paris: The Children of God, 22 December 1971. 5 pp.

169. 150-GP "Have Faith, Will Travel!" London or San Juan: The Children of God, 30 December 1971. 34 pp.

170. 151-LTA "Reading, Pinups, Mistakes & World Conquest!—Thru' Love!" London or San Juan: The Children of God, 26 January 1972. 14 pp.

171. 152-GP "A Psalm of David." London or Paris: The Children of God, 20 January 1972. 8 pp.

172. 153-GP "Let the Dead Bury the Dead!" London or San Juan: The Children of God, 31 January 1972. 5 pp.

173. 154-LTA "A Wonderful Wave of Worldwide Witnessing." London or San Juan: the Children of God, 16 February 1972. 20 pp.

174. 154A-DFO "Faith's Lost Sheep Prophecies." London or San Juan: The Children of God, 30 December 1971. 3 pp.

175. 154B-GP "My Love Is the Wild Wind." London or San Juan: The Children of God, 16 February 1972. 3 pp.

176. 155-LTA "The Laws of Moses." London or San Juan: The Children of God, 21 February 1972. 26 pp.

177. 156-GP "The 70-Years Prophecy of the End." London or Paris: The Children of God, 1 March 1972. 8 pp.

178. 156A-LTA "Corrections." London or San Juan: The Children of God, 12 March 1972. 4 pp.

179. 156B-DO "Advice on Publications." London or San Juan: The Children of God, 17 March 1972. 5 pp.

180. 156C-LTA "Dear Ho and Faith." London or San Juan: The Children of God, 17 March 1972. 5 pp.

181. 157-LTA "Thanks and Comments." London or San Juan: The Children of God, 23 March 1972. 10 pp.

182. 158-LT "The Almond Tree." London or San Juan: The Children of God, 18 March 1972. 5 pp.

183. 159-GP "Be So Happy!" London or San Juan: The Children of God, 7 April 1972. 8 pp.

184. 160-GP "The Great Escape!" London or San Juan: The Children of God, 24 April. 8 pp.

185. 160A-GP "The Emergency!" London or San Juan: The Children of God, 24 April 1972. 4 pp.

186. 160B-LTO "Flee as a Bird!" London or San Juan: The Children of God, 24 April 1972. 4 pp.

187. 161-LTA "Labour Leaders." London or San Juan: The Children of God, 5 May 1972. 10 pp.

188. 162-GP "Mene, Mene, Tekel, Upharsin!" London or Paris: The Children of God, 10 May 1972. 10 pp.

189. 163-LTA "Dreams of Jeremiah 40." London or San Juan: The Children of God, 25 May 1972. 7 pp.

190. 164-GP "Operations P.A.C.C." London or San Juan: The Children of God, 26 May 1972. 7 pp.

191. 165-GP "The School." Paris or London: The Children of God, 28 May 1972. 5 pp.

192.   166-DO "The Music That Made the Revolution." London or San Juan: The Children of God, 28 May 1972. 3 pp.

193.   167-GP "Other Sheep." London or Paris: The Children of God, 1 June 1972. 12 pp.

194.   168-LTA "Baalzebub—Lord of the Flies." London or San Juan: The Children of God, 12 June 1972. 8 pp.

195.   168A-LTA "Emergency Notice to All—Leaders of All Colonies!" London or San Juan: The Children of God, 12 June 1972. 3 pp.

196.   169-GP "My Yoke Is Easy!" London or San Juan: The Children of God, 12 June 1972. 3 pp.

197.   170-GP "Vanity Fair!" London or Paris: The Children of God, 13 June 1972. 7 pp.

198.   171-GP "Attack!" London or Paris: The Children of God, 20 June 1972. 9 pp.

199.   172-GP "Survival!" London or Paris: The Children of God, June 1972. 51 pp.

200.   173-GP "Your Declaration of Independence!" London or San Juan: The Children of God, 4 July 1972. 4 pp.

201.   174-GP "99 Theses." London or Paris: The Children of God, July 1972. 3 pp.

202.   175-DO "The Monster!" London or San Juan: The Children of God, 19 July 1972. 10 pp.

203.   176-DO "Monster on the Move!" London or San Juan: The Children of God, 15 August 1972. 14 pp.

204.   177-GP "Call of India." London or San Juan: The Children of God, 10 September 1972. 5 pp.

205.   178-LTA "Border Bases." London or San Juan: The Children of God, 9 September 1972. 3 pp.

206.   179-GP "Are the Children of God a Sect?" London or San Juan: The Children of God, 10 September 1972. 1 p.

207.   179A-GP "Are You a Good Sport?" London or Paris: The Children of God, September 1972. 3 pp.

208.   180-LTA "Arrivederci Roma!" London or San Juan: The Children of God, September 1972. 8 pp.

209.   181-LTA "Prayer for a Queen." London or San Juan: The Children of God, 16 September 1972. 7 pp.

210.   182-GP "Die Daily!" London or San Juan: The Children of God, September 1972. 5 pp.

211. 183-LTA "The World Council of Churches." London or San Juan: The Children of God, September 1972. 4 pp.

212. 184-GP "Are We Catholics or Protestants?" London or San Juan: The Children of God, September 1972. 9 pp.

213. 185-DO "The Kingdom!" London or San Juan: The Children of God, 1 October 1972. 7 pp.

214. 186-LTA "Prayer for the Prime Minister." London or San Juan: The Children of God, 8 October 1972. 4 pp.

215. 186A-GP "The Watch." London or San Juan: The Children of God, 8 October 1972. 3 pp.

216. 187-GP "802 South." London or San Juan: The Children of God, 23 October 1972. 6 pp.

217. 188-GP "A Prophecy Against Our Enemies!" London or Paris: The Children of God, October 1972. 3 pp.

218. 189-LTA "Mo's Newsletter and Advisory." London or San Juan: The Children of God, November 1972. 8 pp.

219. 190-DO "Newsletter and Advisory—II." London or San Juan: The Children of God, December 1972. 9 pp.

220. 191-GP "Temple Time." London or Paris: The Children of God, December 1972. 9 pp.

221. 192-GP "Papal Audience." London or Paris: The Children of God, 4 October 1972. 6 pp.

222. 193-GP "An Open Letter to Our Friends." London or Paris: The Children of God, 20 December 1972. 6 pp.

223. 194-GP "Spirit Tree!" London or Paris: The Children of God, 20 December 1972. 3 pp.

224. 195-DO "Snowman." London or San Juan: The Children of God, 26 December 1972. 8 pp.

225. 196-GP "Paper Agape!" London or Paris: The Children of God, 1 January 1972. 2 pp.

226. 197-GP "State of the Nation." London or Paris: The Children of God, January 1973. 5 pp.

227. 198-GP "Don Quixote." London or Paris: The Children of God, January 1973. 6 pp.

228. 199-GP "Howard Hughes." London or Paris: The Children of God, January 1973. 5 pp.

229. 200-GP "The Maryknoll Fathers." London or San Juan: The Children of God, 20 January 1973. 2 pp.

230.   201-LTA "The African Nightmare!" London or San Juan: The Children of
       God, 29 January 1973. 4 pp.

231.   202-LTA "The Maharishi of Hyderabad." London or San Juan: The
       Children of God, 30 January 1973. 3 pp.

232.   203-GP "Bell, Book and Candle." London or San Juan: The Children of
       God, February 1973. 9 pp.

233.   204-GP "The Rape of England." London or San Juan: The Children of
       God, January 1973. 3 pp.

234.   205-GP "The Meek." London or San Juan: The Children of God, February
       1973. 4 pp.

235.   206-GP "Heidi." London or San Juan: The Children of God, 18 February
       1973. 4 pp.

236.   207-GP "Wonder Working Words." London or San Juan: The Children of
       God, 28 February 1973. 7 pp.

237.   208-GP "Become One!" London or Paris: The Children of God, 6 March
       1973. 4 pp.

238.   209-DO "Brave Pioneers!" London or San Juan: The Children of God,
       February 1973. 3 pp.

239.   210-LTA "The Office of a Biship." London or San Juan: The Children of
       God, 9 March 1973. 12 pp.

240.   211-DO "Rags to Riches!" London or San Juan: The Children of God, 4
       March 1973. 11 pp.

241.   212-DO "Kings!" London or San Juan: The Children of God, March 1973.
       12 pp.

242.   213-LTA "The Baby." London or San Juan: The Children of God, March
       1973. 4 pp.

243.   214-GP "The Crystal Pyramid!" London or Paris: The Children of God,
       March 1973. 9 pp.

244.   214A-GP "The Amerikan Way." London or San Juan: The Children of
       God, 25 January 1973. 9 pp.

245.   215-LTA "The Birthday Warning!" London or San Juan: The Children of
       God, 18 February 1973. 15 pp.

246.   216-GP "America the Whore!" London or San Juan: The Children of God,
       17 March 1973. 9 pp.

247.   217-LTA "Problem Kings!" London or San Juan: The Children of God,
       March 1973. 6 pp.

248.   218-LTA "Rules for Rulers." London or San Juan: The Children of God,
       April 1973. 5 pp.

249. 219-GP "Special Police Powers." London or San Juan: The Children of God, April 1973. 2 pp.

250. 220-GP "The Flood." London or San Juan: The Children of God, April 1973. 2 pp.

251. 221-GP "The Asylum." London or San Juan: The Children of God, March 1973. 4 pp.

252. 222-GP "The Playground." London or Paris: The Children of God, April 1973. 1 p.

253. 223-GP "The Index." London or San Juan: The Children of God, April 1973. 1 p.

254. 224-LTA "The Goddesses." London or Paris: The Children of God, April 1973. 4 pp.

255. 225-GP "Brother Sun." London or Paris: The Children of God, April 1973. 6 pp.

256. 226-GP "Gaddafi's Magic Lamp." London or Paris: The Children of God, April 1973. 9 pp.

257. 227-DO "The Spiders' Web." London or San Juan: The Children of God, May 1973. 4 pp.

258. 228-GP "Shangri-La—Lost Horizon Found!" London or San Juan: The Children of God, May 1973. 5 pp.

259. 229-LTA "Mo Letter Reprinting List." London or San Juan: The Children of God. 3 pp.

260. 230-GP "Makarios." London or Paris: The Children of God, May 1973. 4 pp.

261. 231-DO "Bye, Bye, Birdie!" London or San Juan: The Children of God, May 1973. 7 pp.

262. 232-GP "Bye, Bye, Pie!" London or Paris: The Children of God, May 1973. 8 pp.

263. 233-LTA "Fed My Sheep!" London or San Juan: The Children of God, February 1973. 2 pp.

264. 234-GP "Aaron on the Mountain." London or Paris: The Children of God, May 1973. 2 pp.

265. 235-GP "The Rose." London or San Juan: the Children of God, 22 March 1973. 3 pp.

266. 236-GP "The Art of Oh!" London or San Juan: The Children of God, 23 January 1973. 1 p.

267. 237-GP "Holy Holes!" London or San Juan: The Children of God, 1 April 1973. 7 pp.

268. 238-GP "Choice." London or Paris: The Children of God, May 1973. 4
      pp.

269. 239-GP "Lampton on the Alter of Watergate." London or Paris: The
      Children of God, 29 May 1973. 3 pp.

270. 240-GP "Mountain Maid!" London or San Juan: The Children of God, 27
      December 1970. 4 pp.

271. 241-DO "Shiners?--Or Shamers!" London or San Juan: The Children of
      God, 26 June 1973. 8 pp.

272. 242-DO "Old Bottles." London or San Juan: The Children of God, July
      1973. 17 pp.

273. 243-GP "The Green Paper Pig." London or Paris: The Children of God,
      23 June 1973. 11 pp.

274. 244-GP "Despise Not Prophesying!" London or Paris: The Children of
      God, 27 June 1973. 6 pp.

275. 245-GP "Gaddafi's Third World!" London or Paris: The Children of God,
      7 July 1973. 8 pp.

276. 246-LTA "Gaddafi--And the Children of God!" London or San Juan: The
      Children of God, 11 June 1973. 10 pp.

277. 247-LTA "Gaddafi's March." London or San Juan: The Children of God,
      20 July 1973. 2 pp.

278. 248-LTA "More on Gaddafi!" London or San Juan: The Children of God,
      7 June 1973. 2 pp.

279. 249-GP "One Wife." London or San Juan: The Children of God, 28
      October 1972. 5 pp.

280. 250-GP "Revolutionary Women." London or San Juan: The Children of
      God, 20 June 1973. 15 pp.

281. 251-DO "New Bottles." London or San Juan: The Children of God, 28
      June 1973. 13 pp.

282. 252-DO "A Prayer in the Spirit." London or San Juan: The Children of
      God, 2 August 1973. 3 pp.

283. 253-DO "Conferences, Colonies, Bands and Buses!" London or San Juan:
      The Children of God, 15 July 1973. 14 pp.

284. 254-DO "Golden Seed!" London or San Juan: The Children of God, 20
      July 1973. 5 pp.

285. 255-GP "War and Peace." London or Paris: The Children of God, 16
      April 1973. 17 pp.

286. 256-GP "Ask Any Communist." London or Paris: The Children of God,
      21 August 1973. 3 pp.

287. 257-GP "The Anti-'God War'! London or Paris: The Children of God, 21 August 1973. 1 p.

288. 258-GP "Revolutionary Sex." London or Paris: The Children of God, 27 March 1973. 28 pp.

289. 259-GP "Revolutionary Love-Making!" London or San Juan: The Children of God, Summer 1970. 13 pp.

290. 260-DFO "Revolutionary Marriage!" London or San Juan: The Children of God, August 1973. 22 pp.

291. 261-DO "Oplexicon!" London or San Juan: The Children of God, 11 July 1973. 5 pp.

292. 262-GP "The Green Door." London or Paris: The Children of God, 29 August, 1973. 17 pp.

293. 263-GP "The Wise and Unwise Leader." London or Paris: The Children of God, 20 August 1973. 11 pp.

294. 264-GP "I Am a Toilet—Are You?" London or Paris: The Children of God, 8 September 1972. 11 pp.

295. 265-DFO "Follow God."

   Corresponds to item 23.

296. 266-GP "The Drug Store." London or Paris: The Children of God, 4 September 1973. 3 pp.

297. 267-DFO "The MO Letter Index Volume I." n.p.: The Children of God, August 1973.

298. 268-GP "Madame M." London or Paris: The Children of God, 25 April 1973. 9 pp.

299. 269-GP "The Christmas Monster!" London or Paris: The Children of God, 8 September 1973. 4 pp.

300. 270-GP "State of the World." London or Paris: The Children of God, September 1973. 10 pp.

301. 271-GP "Solaris." London or Paris: The Children of God, 17 September 1973. 11 pp.

302. 271B "More on Solaris." London or Paris: The Children of God, September 1973. 9 pp.

303. 272-GP "The End of Allende?" London or Paris: The Children of God, 26 Spetember 1973. 12 pp.

304. 273-GP "Chinese Spirits." London or Paris: The Children of God, 30 September 1973. 3 pp.

305. 274-GP "The Arab Wall." London or Paris: The Children of God, 6
      October 1973. 10 pp.

306. 274A-DFO "Warning on Distribution of Controversial Literature!"
      London or Paris: the Children of God, 19 October 1973. 2 pp.

307. 275-GP "The Frog." London or Paris: The Children of God, 16 October
      1973. 21 pp.

308. 275A-DFO "Demonography." London or Paris: The Children of God, 7
      October 1973. 8 pp.

309. 276-GP "The Phoenix." London or Paris: The Children of God, 21
      October 1973. 9 pp.

310. 277-GP "The Real War Goes On!" London or Paris: The Children of God,
      28 October 1973. 16 pp.

311. 278-GP "More on Kohoutek!" London or Paris: The Children of God, 4
      November 1973. 4 pp.

312. 279-GP "Ivan Ivanovitch." London or Paris: The Children of God, 8
      October 1973. 8 pp.

313. 280-GP "40 Days!" London or Paris: The Children of God, 12 November
      1973. 4 pp.

314. 281-GP "Israel Invaded!" London or Paris: The Children of God, 25
      November 1973. 9 pp.

315. 282-GP "Europa." London or San Juan: The Children of God, 19
      November 1973. 5 pp.

316. 282A-DFO "Interpretation." London or Paris: The Children of God, 2
      December 1973. 10 pp.

317. 283-GP "The Comet Comes!" London or Paris: The Children of God, 20
      December 1973. 4 pp.

318. 283A-DO "Contracts." London or San Juan: The Children of God, 26
      October 1973. 2 pp.

319. 284-GP "The Crash!" London or Paris: The Children of God, 16
      December 1973. 8 pp.

320. 285-GP "Psychic Sees the Future!" London or Paris: The Children of
      God, 22 December 1973. 7 pp.

321. 286-GP "Come on Ma!—Burn Your Bra!" London or San Juan: The
      Children of God, 22 December 1973. 4 pp.

322. 287-GP "Jealousy." London or Dallas: The Children of God, September
      1973. 3 pp.

323. 288-GP "Kennedy." London or Paris: The Children of God, 22 December
      1973. 2 pp.

324. 289-GP "More War!" London or Paris: The Children of God, 6 January 1974. 5 pp.

325. 290-GP "Alice and the Magic Garden." London or Paris: The Children of God, 4 December 1972. 11 pp.

326. 291-DO "Bewitched!" London or San Juan: The Children of God, 9 January 1974. 7 pp.

327. 292-GP "Women in Love." London or San Juan: The Children of God, 20 December 1973. 13 pp.

328. 293-DFO "The Little Flirty Fishy." London or San Juan: The Children of God, 3 January 1974. 8 pp.

329. 294-GP "The Money Explodes!" London or San Juan: The Children of God, 24 January 1974. 7 pp.

330. 295-GP "The Comet's Tale." London or Paris: The Children of God, 24 January 1974. 8 pp.

331. 296-GP "Abrahim the Gypsy King!" Paris or London: The Children of God, 30 April 1970. 4 pp.

332. 297-GP "Getting Organized." London or Paris: The Children of God, 15 August 1973. 11 pp.

333. 298-GP "Abrahim" 'The Gypsies' Story!'" London or San Juan: The Children of God, 30 April 1970. 5 pp.

334. 299-GP "Students Stand Up!" London or San Juan: The Children of God, 28 January 1974. 3 pp.

335. 300-DFO "The MO Letter Index Volume II." n.p., January 1974.

336. 301-GP "How Arabs Became Gypsies!" London or San Juan: The Children of God, 20 December 1970. 5 pp.

337. 301A-DO "Share the Know!" London or San Juan: The Children of God, February 1974. 8 pp.

338. 301B-DO "To My 'Typewriter Queens'!" London or San Juan: The Children of God, 1 February 1974. 2 pp.

339. 301C-DO "Lord Byron's Surrender." London or San Juan: The Children of God, 2 March 1974. 3 pp.

340. 302-GP "Prayer Power!" London or San Juan: The Children of God, 29 May 1972. 4 pp.

341. 302A-DFO "The 'All Things' Tree." London or San Juan: The Children of God, 21 March 1974. 2 pp.

342. 302B-DFO "Aries—The Ram." London or San Juan: The Children of God, March 1974. 2 pp.

343. 302C-DO "The Law of Love!" London or San Juan: The Children of God, 21 March 1974. 3 pp.

344. 303-GP "Exorcism." London or San Juan: The Children of God, April 1974. 7 pp.

345. 303A-DFO "Paper Power." London or Paris: The Children of God, 10 February 1974. 14 pp.

346. 304-GP "Look of Love." London or San Juan: The Children of God, 1 April 1974. 8 pp.

347. 305-GP "Que Sera', Sera'!--Preface." London or San Juan: The Children of God, 25 May 1974. 1 p.

348. 306-GP "Sex Works!" London or San Juan: The Children of God, 2 June 1974. 14 pp.

349. 307-GP "Lovelight!" London or San Juan: The Children of God, 24 June 1974. 9 pp.

350. 307A-DFO "To Our Worldwide Family!" London or San Juan: The Children of God, July 1974. 4 pp.

351. 307B-DFO "The Antenna." London or San Juan: The Children of God, 1 September 1972. 4 pp.

352. 308-GP "Revolutionary Love Letters and Poems." n.p., July 1974.

353. 309-GP "Beauty and the Beasts." London or San Juan: The Children of God, 7 April 1974. 11 pp.

354. 309A-LTA "The Sword of the Lord!" London or San Juan: The Children of God, 18 July 1974. 4 pp.

355. 309B-DFO "Builders Beware!" London or San Juan: The Children of God, 25 July 1974. 8 pp.

356. 310-GP "World-Famed Economists Forecast Doom!" London or San Juan: The Children of God, 28 August 1974. 5 pp.

357. 310A-LTA "Mo's Worldwide Newsletter No. 1." London or San Juan: The Children of God, August 1974. 3 pp.

358. 310B-LTA "Mo's Worldwide Newsletter No. 2." London or San Juan: The Children of God, 9 August 1974. 3 pp.

359. 311-GP "How To Survive War!" London or San Juan: The Children of God, September 1974. 6 pp.

360. 311A-DFO "Lovest Thou Me?" London or San Juan: The Children of God, July 1974. 12 pp.

361. 311B-DFO "Hitch Your Wagon To a Star!" London or San Juan: The Children of God, 8 September 1974. 5 pp.

362. 311C-DFO "Mo's Worldwide Family Newsletters No. 6, 7 & 8." London or San Juan: the Children of God, June 1974. 11 pp.

363. 312A-LTA "Mo's Worldwide Family Newsletter No. 9." London or San Juan: the Children of God, 30 August 1974. 4 pp.

364. 312B-DFO "Mo's Worldwide Family Newsletter No. 10, 11 & 12." London or San Juan: The Children of God, September 1974. 11 pp.

365. 312C-DFO "Inspired and Uninspired Songs." London or San Juan: The Children of God, 31 July 1974. 5 pp.

    Duplicates item 116.

366. 313-GP "But if Not.... !" London or San Juan: The Children of God, 13 September 1974. 10 pp.

367. 313B-DO "France Our Friend!" London or San Juan: The Children of God, 8 October 1974. 4 pp.

368. 313C-DFO "Backsliding." London or San Juan: The Children of God, October 1974. 5 pp.

369. 314-GP "Revolutionary New Life!" London or San Juan: The Children of God, June 1974. 3 pp.

370. 314A-DFO "Forsaking All." London or San Juan: The Children of God, October 1974. 3 pp.

371. 314B-LTO "Marriage Problems!" London or San Juan: The Children of God, 10 August 1974. 4 pp.

372. 314C-DFO "Reports and Moving!" London or San Juan: The Children of God, 1 August 1974. 9 pp.

373. 315-GP "What Is That in Thy Hand?" London or San Juan: The Children of God, 4 October 1974. 10 pp.

374. 315A-DFO "Telephone Traitors and Problem Pastors!" London or San Juan: the Children of God, 3 October 1974. 7 pp.

375. 315B-LT "The Blob War!" London or San Juan: The Children of God, 3 October 1974. 7 pp.

376. 315C-DFO "Indigenous!" London or San Juan: The Children of God, 17 October 1974. 6 pp.

377. 316-GP "Heavenly Homes!" London or San Juan: The Children of God, 21 October 1974. 4 pp.

378. 316A-DFO "The Birds and the Seeds!" London or San Juan: The Children of God, 18 October 1974. 12 pp.

379. 316B-DFO "The Blob Story!" London or San Juan: The Children of God, 19 October 1974. 12 pp.

380. 316C-DFO "Know the Share." London or San Juan: The Children of God, 21 October 1974. 4 pp.

381. 317-GP "The Truth!" London or San Juan: The Children of God, 3 November 1974. 6 pp.

382. 317A-DFO "Credits, Designations, Sharing & Rewards." London or San Juan: the Children of God, 30 October 1974. 5 pp.

383. 317B-DFO "Fret Not!" London or San Juan: The Children of God, 1 November 1974. 6 pp.

384. 317C-DO "Mo's World Wide Family Newsletter No. 23." London or San Juan: the Children of God, 27 October 1974. 5 pp.

385. 318-GP "Scatteration!" London or San Juan: The Children of God, March 1971. 18 pp.

386. 318B-DFO "Local Pubs!" London or San Juan: The Children of God, 4 November 1974. 8 pp.

387. 318C-DO "Family News!--Mo's Worldwide Family Newsletter No. 25." London or San Juan: The Children of God, 13 November 1974. 13 pp.

388. 319-GP "The Tree." London or San Juan: The Children of God, October 1974. 11 pp.

389. 320-GP "Listening?--Or Lamenting?" London or San Juan: The Children of God, 17 November 1974. 11 pp.

390. 321-GP "Rich Man, Poor Man." London or San Juan: The Children of God, 11 November 1974. 16 pp.

391. 322-GP "A Child's Story of Blobs!" London or San Juan: The Children of God, 28 November 1974. 12 pp.

392. 322A-DFO "Mo's Worldwide Family Newsletter No. 26." London or San Juan: the Children of God, 1 January 1975. 3 pp.

393. 323-GP "The Dancer." London or San Juan: The Children of God, 16 January 1974. 5 pp.

394. 324-GP "The City of Buried Treasure." London or San Juan: The Children of God, 27 December 1974. 7 pp.

395. 325-GP "Letter to a Labourer." London or San Juan: The Children of God, 20 January 1975. 3 pp.

396. 325A-DFO "The Oh of Art!" London or San Juan: The Children of God, 15 January 1975. 8 pp.

397. 325B-DFO "The Round Round Room." London or San Juan: The Children of God, 19 January 1975. 5 pp.

398. 325C-DFO "The Japanese--South American Dream." London or San Juan: the Children of God, 27 January 1975. 9 pp.

399. 326-GP "Musical Key." London or San Juan: The Children of God, 12 May 1973. 7 pp.

400. 326A-DFO "Sequel to 'Musical Key.'" London or San Juan: The Children of God, 1 January 1975. 4 pp.

401. 326B-DFO "Fair Sex." London or San Juan: The Children of God, February 1975. 4 pp.

402. 326C-LT "How to Survive in a Small Colony." London or San Juan: The Children of God, 24 October 1974. 4 pp.

403. 327-GP "Inflation or Deflation?" London or San Juan: The Children of God, 9 December 1974. 6 pp.

404. 328-GP "Glamour or Glory?" London or San Juan: The Children of God, 30 March 1973. 10 pp.

405. 328A-DFO "The Lit Revolution!" London or San Juan: The Children of God, 17 February 1975. 5 pp.

406. 328B-DFO "The Disciple Revolution!" London or San Juan: The Children of God, 18 February 1975. 9 pp.

407. 328C-LT "The Shake-Up!" London or San Juan: The Children of God, 18 February 1975. 10 pp.

408. 329-GP "The Word—New and Old." London or San Juan: The Children of God, September 1974. 4 pp.

409. 329A-LTO "The Bloodless Coup!" London or San Juan: The Children of God, 18 February 1975. 4 pp.

410. 329B-DFO "The Colony Revolution!" London or San Juan: The Children of God. 10 pp.

411. 329C-DO "The New Leadership Revolution!" London or San Juan: The Children of God, March 1975. 7 pp.

412. 330-GP "Our Message." London or San Juan: The Children of God, September 1974. 5 pp.

413. 330A-LTO "The Economy Revolution!" London or San Juan: The Children of God, 15 March 1975. 12 pp.

414. 330B-LTO "The Childcare Revolution!" London or San Juan: The Children of God, 1 April 1975. 7 pp.

415. 330C-DFO "What's the Difference?" London or San Juan: The Children of God, 1 February 1975. 7 pp.

416. 331-GP "The Early Church." London or Paris: The Children of God, August 1974. 10 pp.

417. 331A-LTO "Prophecies of the Great Queen." London or Paris: The Children of God, 27 July 1971. 10 pp.

418. 331B-LTO "How To!" London or Paris: The Children of God, 2 March
      1975. 11 pp.

419. 331C-LTO "More on 'How To.'" London or Paris: The Children of God,
      28 March 1975. 10 pp.

420. 332-GP "The Church System." London or Paris: The Children of God,
      August 1974. 4 pp.

421. 332A-LTO "What To." London or Paris: The Children of God, 28 March
      1975. 10 pp.

422. 332B-LTO "When To!" London or San Juan: The Children of God, March
      1975. 10 pp.

423. 332C-DO "Sex Problems!" London or San Juan: The Children of God, 3
      March 1975. 13 pp.

424. 333-GP "The Political System." London or Paris: The Children of God,
      September 1974. 6 pp.

425. 333A-DFO "Rolled Gold." London or Paris: The Children of God, 9
      February 1975. 7 pp.

426. 333B-DFO "Eritrea!" London or Paris: The Children of God, 24 February
      1975. 3 pp.

427. 333C-DFO "Registration?--Or Scatteration!" London or Paris: The
      Children of God, 4 February 1975. 3 pp.

428. 334-GP "The End-Time Whispering Vision." London or Paris: The
      Children of God, April 1975. 19 pp.

429. 334A-DFO "Who To!--Pushers or Problems?" London or San Juan: The
      Children of God, 22 April 1975. 23 pp.

430. 334B-DFO "Explosion!" London or San Juan: The Children of God, May
      1975. 5 pp.

431. 334C-LTO "Where To!" London or San Juan: The Children of God, 8
      March 1975. 7 pp.

432. 335-GP "Who Is Moses Colouring Book." n.p., March 1975.

433. 335A-DFO "The Holy War!" London or San Juan: The Children of God,
      May 1975. 5 pp.

434. 335B-DO "Amenuensis." London or San Juan: The COG, 22 November
      1973. 12 pp.

435. 335C-DO "The French Connection!" London or San Juan: The Children
      of God, June 1975. 5 pp.

436. 336A-LTO "Pickin' Up the Pieces!" London or San Juan: The Children of
      God, 27 June 1975. 7 pp.

437. 336B-DO "100-Fold!" London or San Juan: The Children of God, August 1975. 8 pp.

438. 336C-DO "Brunheld." London or San Juan: The Children of God, 19 July 1975. 2 pp.

439. 337-GP "The Spirit of God." n.p.: The Children of God, 28 August 1974. 4 pp.

440. 337A-DFO "Ordination." London or San Juan: The Children of God, 30 March 1975. 6 pp.

441. 337B-DFO "Communion." London or San Juan: The Children of God, 30 March 1975. 6 pp.

442. 337C-DFO "Boat Travel!" London or San Juan: The Children of God, 11 January 1975. 4 pp.

443. 338-GP "Naming the Baby!" London or San Juan: The Children of God, 7 February 1975. 15 pp.

444. 339-GP "The Deluge!" London or San Juan: The Children of God, 2 March 1975. 6 pp.

445. 340-GP "The Hamburger Boat!" London or San Juan: The Children of God, 16 March 1975. 6 pp.

446. 341-GP "Spiritual Communications." London or San Juan: The Children of God, September 1975. 11 pp.

447. 3420-GP "The Challenge of Godahfi." London or San Juan: The Children of God, June 1975. 3 pp.

448. 343-GP "Daniel II." London or Paris: The Children of God, April 1975. 7 pp.

449. 344-GP "Witnessing!" London or Paris: The Children of God, 16 April 1975. 5 pp.

450. 345-GP "The Name of Jesus!" London or Paris: The Children of God, 16 April 1975. 5 pp.

451. 346-GP "Daniel 7." London: The Children of God, May 1975. 6 pp.

452. 347-GP "Daniel 8." London: The Children of God, June 1975. 7 pp.

453. 348-GP "Daniel 9." Paris: The Children of God, July 1975. 7 pp.

454. 349-GP "Daniel 10, 11 & 12." Rome: The Children of God, August 1975. 11 pp.

455. 350-GP "The World Today!" n.p.: The Children of God, 2 August 1975. 15 pp.

456. 351-GP "Our Shepherd, Moses David." Rome: The Children of God, January 1976. 15 pp.

457.   352-DO "The Uneager Beaver." n.p.: The Children of God, 14 October 1975. 11 pp.

458.   353-GP "Mo's Pointers for Health!" n.p.: The Children of God, April 1975. 34 pp.

459.   354-DFO "The Sinking Boat Dream." n.p.: The Children of God, 6 October 1975. 7 pp.

460.   355-GP "The U.S.-Merchant Submarine Dream." n.p.: The Children of God, 7 May 1975. 11 pp.

461.   356-LT "35 MM Negs!" Italy: The Children of God, 13 July 1975. 3 pp.

462.   357-DO "Administration Revolution!" Rome: The Children of God, 11 November 1975. 8 pp.

463.   358-GP "The Secret Weapon." n.p.: The Children of God, 17 November 1975. 3 pp.

464.   359-DFO "Divorce—The Marriage Revolution!" n.p.: The Children of God, 25 November 1975. 5 pp.

465.   360-GP "Strange Truths!" n.p.: The Children of God, 23 July 1975. 7 pp.

466.   361-DFO "The Crystal Stream." n.p.: The Children of God, 6 November 1975. 2 pp.

467.   362-DO "The Old Phonograph!" n.p.: The Children of God, 6 November 1975. 2 pp.

468.   363-DFO "The Halloween Wheel." n.p.: The Children of God, 31 October 1975. 8 pp.

469.   364A-LT "Security in God's Kingdom." n.p.: The Children of God, 24 October 1975. 3 pp.

470.   364B-LT "The Pier." n.p.: The Children of God, 8 December 1975. 2 pp.

471.   365-GP "The Dark Kingdom!" n.p.: The Children of God, 31 July 1975. 6 pp.

472.   366-DFO "Poison in Paradise!" n.p.: The Children of God, 16 November 1975. 4 pp.

473.   367-DFO "The Empty Wind." n.p.: The Children of God, 14 June 1975. 7 pp.

474.   368-GP "Where Poppies Grow." n.p.: The Children of God, 22 December 1975. 7 pp.

475.   369-GP "Prayer." n.p.: The Children of God, May 1975. 2 pp.

476.   370-GP "Pawn." n.p.: The Children of God, 25 August 1975. 4 pp.

477. 371-DFO "The Education Revolution!" n.p.: The Children of God, November 1975. 9 pp.

478. 372-GP "The American Holocaust!" n.p.: The Children of God, January 1976. 8 pp.

479. 373-GP "Death to the Cities!" n.p.: The Children of God, 30 November 1975. 18 pp.

480. 374-DFO "The Bloodsuckers!" n.p.: The Children of God, 20 September 1975. 6 pp.

481. 375-GP "Grandmother and the Flood!" n.p.: The Children of God, 20 October 1974. 2 pp.

482. 376-GP "There Are Absolutes!" n.p.: The Children of God, 28 December 1975. 5 pp.

483. 377-LTO "New Appointments!" n.p.: The Children of God, 6 December 1975. 4 pp.

484. 378-GP "The Bomb Dreams!" n.p.: The Children of God, January 1976. 4 pp.

485. 379-DO "Flee the City!" n.p.: The Children of God, 20 October 1974. 3 pp.

486. 380-DFO "More U.S. Nightmares!" n.p.: The Children of God, 21 October 1974. 3 pp.

487. 381-DO "The Last American Nightmare?" n.p.: The Children of God, 11 April 1975. 4 pp.

488. 382-DFO "Happy New 1976!" n.p.: The Children of God, January 1976. 6 pp.

489. 383-DFO "The Frozen Book!" n.p.: The Children of God, 23 January 1976. 5 pp.

490. 384-DFO "Desperate Prayer." n.p.: The Children of God, 28 October 1975. 2 pp.

491. 385-GP "Letter to America." n.p.: The Children of God, February 1976. 19 pp.

492. 386-DFO "Gotcher 'Flee Bag'?" n.p.: The Children of God, 14 January 1976. 19 pp.

493. 387-GP "Pat Price." n.p.: The Children of God, 19 September 1975. 3 pp.

494. 388-DO "Sahara." n.p.: The Children of God, 28 October 1975. 4 pp.

495. 389-DFO "Real Mothers!" n.p.: The Children of God, 18 November 1975. 12 pp.

496.   390-DO "The Angola Dream." n.p.: The Children of God, 4 January
        1976. 2 pp.

497.   391-GP "The Battle for Africa!" n.p.: The Children of God, 16 February
        1976. 15 pp.

498.   392-GP "The Conakry Rip-Off!" n.p.: The Children of God, 22 February
        1976. 5 pp.

499.   393-GP "The Trans-Iberian Canal." n.p.: The Children of God, 26
        February 1976. 5 pp.

500.   394-GP "Mo Meets Mo' Amar Godahfi!" n.p.: The Children of God, 16
        June 1975. 15 pp.

501.   395-DO "Days of Heaven." n.p.: The Children of God, 10 November
        1975. 7 pp.

502.   396-GP "The Land of Not Too Much." n.p.: The Children of God, 3
        February 1976. 2 pp.

503.   397-GP "They Behold His Face!" n.p.: The Children of God, 20 January
        1976. 2 pp.

504.   398-GP "Revelation 1-7." Rome: The Children of God, February 1976.
        15 pp.

505.   399-GP "Mo's Music!" n.p.: The Children of God, 31 August 1971. 23 pp.

506.   400-GP "The Children's Crusade!" n.p.: The Children of God, 28 May
        1971. 3 pp.

507.   501-DFO "King Arthur's Nights!—Chapter 1: The Night Crawlers!" and
        "Chapter 2: The Cost of Flirty Fishing!" n.p.: The Children of God, 29
        April 1976. 8 pp.

508.   502-DFO "King Arthur's Nights!—Chapter 3: King Meets King!" and
        "Chapter 4: the Odd Couple!" n.p.: The Children of God, 10 May 1976.
        6 pp.

509.   502R-GP "The Family of Love?—Mortal Sin?—or Salvation!" n.p.: The
        Family of Love, June 1977. 4 pp.

510.   503-DFO "King Arthur's Nights!—Chapter 5: How to Charm a Fish With
        A Flame!" n.p.: The Children of God, 26 January 1974. 8 pp.

511.   504-DFO Newlove, Arthur. "King Arthur's Nights!—Chapter 6: He Tells
        His Own Story!" n.p.: The Children of God, 6 April 1975. 4 pp.

512.   505-DFO "King Arthur's Nights!—Chapter 7: The Hooker!" n.p.: The
        Children of God, 28 February 1974. 8 pp.

513.   506-DFO Newlove, Arthur. "King Arthur's Nights!—Chapter 8: Maria's
        Nights!" n.p.: The Children of God, 6 April 1975. 7 pp.

514. 507-DFO Newlove, Arthur. "King Arthur's Nights!—Chapter 9: Becky's Nights!" n.p.: The Children of God, 6 April 1975. 6 pp.

515. 508-DFO Newlove, Rebecca. "King Arthur's Nights!—Chapter 10: Becky's Own Story!" n.p.: The Children of God, April-May 1974. 3 pp.

516. 509-DFO Newlove, Rebecca. "King Arthur's Nights!—Chapter 11: Hypnotised!" n.p.: The Children of God, May-June 1974. 7 pp.

517. 510-DFO Maria and Moses David. "King Arthur's Nights!—Chapter 12: The Tunnel and the Call to Arms!" n.p.: The Children of God, 22 June 1974. 8 pp.

518. 511-DFO Newlove, Rebecca and Arthur Newlove. "King Arthur's Nights!—Chapter 13: Hooked!" n.p.: The Children of God, June 1974. 8 pp.

519. 512-DFO Newlove, Rebecca and Arthur Newlove. "King Arthur's Nights!—Chapter 14: Seduced!" n.p.: The Children of God, June-July 1974. 8 pp.

520. 513-DFO Maria, Moses David, Rebecca Newlove and Arthur Newlove. "King Arthur's Nights!—Chapter 15: Freed!" n.p.: The Children of God, July 1974. 8 pp.

521. 514-DFO Newlove, Rebecca. "King Arthur's Nights!—Chapter 16: Taming the Baby!" n.p.: The Children of God, July-August 1974. 8 pp.

522. 515-DFO Newlove, Rebecca and Arthur Newlove. "King Arthur's Nights!—Chapter 17: Victory!" n.p.: The Children of God, August 1974. 8 pp.

523. 516-DFO Maria, Moses David, Rebecca Newlove and Arthur Newlove. "King Arthur's Nights!—Chapter 18: Progress!" n.p.: The Children of God, October-November 1974. 8 pp.

524. 517-DFO "King Arthur's Nights!—Chapter 19: The Wizard of Ahs!" n.p.: The Children of God, 7 December 1974. 3 pp.

525. 518-DFO Maria, Moses David, Rebecca Newlove and Arthur Newlove. "King Arthur's Nights!—Chapter 20: New Life!" n.p.: The Children of God, December-January 1975. 6 pp.

526. 519-DFO Newlove, Rebecca, Arthur Newlove and Maria David. "King Arthur's Knights!—Chapter 21: The Birth of a Baby!" n.p.: The Children of God, February-March 1975. 8 pp.

527. 520-GP "Jimmy Carter—America's last chance?" n.p.: The Children of God, 12 June 1976. 3 pp.

528. 521-DFO Newlove, Rebecca and Arthur Newlove. "King Arthur's Nights!—Chapter 22: The Big Fish Becomes the Big Fisherman!" n.p.: The Children of God, April-July 1975. 8 pp.

529. 522-DFO Newlove, Arthur, Becky Newlove and Maria David. "King Arthur's Nights!—Chapter 23: The Odd Couple Return!" n.p.: The Children of God, July 1975-May 1976. 6 pp.

530. 523-GP "The British in Uganda and Strategy in Lebanon." n.p.: The Children of God, 14 July 1976. 4 pp.

531. 524-LTO David, Maria and Moses David. "The One That Got Away!— Part I: on Unsuccessful Flirty-Fishing!" n.p.: The Children of God, 11 March 1974. 7 pp.

532. 525-LTO David, Maria and Moses David. "The One That Got Away!— Part II: Jesus & Sex!" n.p.: The Children of God, 11 March 1974. 8 pp.

533. 526-DFO David, Maria. "Letter to a Lover!" n.p.: The Children of God, 4 August 1976. 6 pp.

534. 527-DFO "F-F'ing!—4 Steps & 7 Proofs of Salvation!" n.p.: The Children of God, 7 June 1976. 7 pp.

535. 528-DO "Rape!—The Violent Take It by Force!" n.p.: The Children of God, 24 April 1974. 7 pp.

536. 529-DO "Male or Female?" n.p.: The Children of God, 9 May 1974. 5 pp.

537. 530-DO "Little Jewels." n.p.: The Children of God, August 1976. 7 pp.

538. 531-GP "Infidelity!" n.p.: The Children of God, 16 August 1976. 2 pp.

539. 532-LTO "The Adventures of a Flirty-Fish!" n.p.: The Children of God, 31 March 1974. 7 pp.

540. 533-DFO "Four Fishing Failures!" n.p.: The Children of God, 6 April 1974. 7 pp.

541. 534-GP "Revelation 8-14." Rome: The Children of God, July 1976. 23 pp.

542. 535-DO "The Little Dog Dream" n.p.: The Children of God, 17 August 1976. 8 pp.

543. 536-DO "Mo' Li'l Jewels!" n.p.: The Children of God, September 1976. 7 pp.

544. 537-DO "God's Love Slave!" n.p.: The Children of God, 21 April 1974. 7 pp.

545. 538-DO "The Ministry of Love!" n.p.: The Children of God, 3 May 1974. 6 pp.

546. 539-DO "Jewels Galore!" n.p.: The Children of God, September 1976. 7 pp.

547. 540-DO "More Precious Pearls!" n.p.: The Children of God, September 1976. 7 pp.

548. 541-GP "Revelation 15-22." Rome: The Children of God, August 1976. 19 pp.

549. 542-DO "Don't Drop Out!—Drop In!" n.p.: The Children of God, 1 August 1976. 14 pp.

550. 543-DO "Feedin' the Fish!" n.p.:the Children of God, 18 May 1975. 1 p.

551. 544-DFO "God's Eyes!" n.p.: The Children of God, 19 July 1976. 6 pp.

552. 545-DO "—Do You Want a 'Penis?—Or a Sword!'" n.p.: The Children of God, 19 July 1976. 5 pp.

553. 546-DRO "Raul's Knife!" n.p.: The Children of God, July 1976. 4 pp.

554. 547-DO "Deep Sea Fishing!" n.p.: The Children of God, 29 May 1976. 11 pp.

555. 548-DO "FF Tips!" n.p.: The Children of God, 4 May 1976. 16 pp.

556. 549-DO "More on Feedin' the Fish!" n.p.: The Children of God, May 1976. 7 pp.

557. 550-DO "Fishin' Fever!" n.p.: The Children of God, May 1976. 7 pp.

558. 551-DFO "Fighters!—What Did You Join the Army For?" n.p.: The Children of God, 21 September 1976. 15 pp.

559. 552-DO "The Bait That Fell in Love with a Fish!" n.p.: The Children of God, 3 May 1976. 8 pp.

560. 553-DO "Teamwork!" n.p.: The Children of God, May 1976. 11 pp.

561. 554-DO "'Mocumba!'—The Conversion of Africa?" n.p.: The Children of God, 21 August 1976. 5 pp.

562. 555-DO "'The Catch!'—More FF Tips!" n.p.: The Children of God, 10 October 1976. 15 pp.

563. 556-DFO "A Missionary's Prayer." n.p.: The Children of God, 17 May 1975. 5 pp.

564. 557-GP "The Snake Charmer!" n.p.: The Children of God, November 1976. 3 pp.

565. 558-GP "'Mo on America': The U.S. Election of Carter." n.p.: The Children of God, 10 November 1976. 1 p.

566. 559-DO "The FFer's Handbook!" n.p.: The Children of God, January 1977. 31 pp.

567. 560-DO "God's Whores?" n.p.: The Children of God, 26 April 1976. 5 pp.

568. 561-DO "The Priestesses of Love!" n.p.: The Children of God, 26 April 1976. 10 pp.

569.   562-DO "FF Coupling!"

570.   563-DO "'FF Behavior!'—More FF Tips!" n.p.: The Children of God,
        December 1976. 5 pp.

571.   564-DO "'The Men Who Play God!'—FF Blues!" n.p.: The Children of
        God, 10 October 1976. 3 pp.

572.   565-GP "Change the World!" n.p.: The Children of God, 5 January 1977.
        10 pp.

573.   566-DFO "Dirty Dishes." n.p.: The Children of God, 22 October 1976. 4
        pp.

574.   567-DO "Pisces: The Age of Tribulation?" n.p.: The Children of God, 26
        April 1976. 2 pp.

575.   568-DFO "Idolsmashers!" n.p.: The Children of God, Summer 1968. 11
        pp.

576.   569-DO "Afflictions." n.p.: The Children of God, 25 November 1976. 26
        pp.

577.   570-DFO "'Nuns of Love.'—The FFer's Declaration of Independence!"
        n.p.: the Children of God, 19 February 1977. 10 pp.

578.   571-DO "Winning the System." n.p.: The Children of God, 25 November
        1976. 5 pp.

579.   572-DO "'The Mothers of God!'—Or 'Don't Give Up the Fish!'" n.p.: The
        Children of God, 19 October 1976. 17 pp.

580.   573-DO "God's Witches!" n.p.: The Children of God, 6 June 1976. 17 pp.

581.   574-DO "The Battle for Katanga & Famagusta!" n.p.: The Children of
        God, 14 April 1977. 11 pp.

582.   575-DO "'The FF Revolution!'—For Strong Volunteers!" n.p.: The
        Children of God, 7 August 1976. 18 pp.

583.   576-DO "The FF Explosion!" n.p.: The Children of God, 6 April 1977. 19
        pp.

584.   577-DFO "'The Wrath of God!'—On Tenerife and Its System's Ugly Face
        Of Tyranny!" n.p.: The Children of God, 5 March 1977. 11 pp.

585.   578-DFO "The Evil Horse!" n.p.: The Children of God, 27 April 1977. 10
        pp.

586.   579-DFO David, Moses and Timothy Concerned. "I'll Be Back!" n.p.: The
        Children of God, 23 March 1977. 11 pp.

587.   580-DFO "Communicate!" n.p.: The Children of God, 25 April 1977. 7
        pp.

588. 581-DO "God's Bosoms!" n.p.: The Children of God, 25 April 1977. 5 pp.

589. 582-GP "'The Children's Dream.'—Or America's Nightmare?" n.p.: The Children of God, 7 March 1977. 4 pp.

590. 583-DO "The Woman with More Mercy Than God!" n.p.: The Children of God, 7 November 1976. 14 pp.

591. 584-GP "My Love Letter—To You!" Hong Kong: Gold Lion Publishers, June 1977. 4 pp.

592. 585-GP "Interviu's 202 Lies!" n.p.: The Children of God, 12 June 1977. 5 pp.

593. 585R-GP "The Anti-God War!" n.p.: The Children of God, June 1977. 5 pp.

594. 586-DFO "Defend the Faith!" n.p.: The Children of God, 20 June 1977. 1 p.

595. 587-DFO Mo and Maria. "'It's a Boy!'—The Story of Baby David!— Chapter 1: 'The Birth of Baby David!'" n.p.: The Children of God, 27 January 1975. 30 pp.

596. 588-DFO "Open the Door for the Children!" n.p.: The Children of God, 31 May 1977. 8 pp.

597. 589-GP "'Our Answers'—To Inteviu's 202 Lies About the Children of God and Family of Love!" n.p.: The Children of God, 12 June 1977. 19 pp.

598. 590-DFO "'Our Replies!'—To the 62 Lies of the Las Palmas Daily of July 8!" n.p.: the Children of God, 17 July 1977. 14 pp.

599. 591-DFO "The 51 Errors of 'Daily Notices'!—Of Santa Cruz, Tenerife, Canary Islands, Spain." n.p.: The Children of God, 24 July 1977. 12 pp.

600. 592-DFO "'God's Only Law Is Love!'—What the Bible says about true free love!" n.p.: The Children of God, 29 July 1977. 5 pp.

601. 593-GP "Our Report to 'Time'—On the False and Forged 'Goodbye' Leaflet." n.p.: the Children of GOd, 2 August 1977. 4 pp.

602. 594-DFO "When Is 'Sin' Not Sin?" n.p.: The Children of God, 8 August 1977. 12 pp.

603. 595-DFO "The Jeane Manson Prayer." n.p.: The Children of God, 19 July 1977. 2 pp.

604. 596-DFO "Late News!" n.p.: The Children of God, 8 August 1977. 15 pp.

605. 597-DFO "How to Take It!" n.p.: The Children of God, 23 August 1977. 11 pp.

606. 598-GP "More Truth!" n.p.: The Children of God, 23 August 1977. 12 pp.

607. 599-DO "Pill?--Or Pilgrimage!" n.p.: The Children of God, 8 August 1977. 27 pp.

608. 600-RVGP "Our Family Symbol." n.p.: The Children of God, August 1977. 1 p.

609. Ashtree, Justus, Cedar Gypsy and Moses David, eds. "Weekly Girly Magazine 'Yes.'" n.p., 4 February 1977. 1 p.

610. Emanuele (translator). "The Day." Hong Kong: The Family of Love, 8 February 1977. 5 pp.

611. Alfred (translator). "The Diary." Hong Kong: The Family of Love, 9 February 1977. 5 pp.

612. Alfred (translator). "The Day." Hong Kong: The Family of Love, 10 February 1977. 5 pp.

613. Ashtree, Justus and Moses David, eds. "The Diary." n.p., May 1977. 10 pp.

614. Ashtree, Justus and Moses David, eds. "The Day." n.p., May 1977. 2 pp.

615. Ashtree, Justus and Moses David, eds. "National Radio Interview." n.p., 22 February 1977. 3 pp.

616. 601-DFO "From Whence Come Wars?" n.p.: The Children of God, September 1978. 9 pp.

617. 602-DO "Lady Luck!" n.p.: The Children of God, September 1977. 20 pp.

618. 603-DO "FF-ing and Jealousy!" n.p: The Children of God, October 1977. 4 pp.

619. 604-DFO "Doubts!" n.p.: The Children of God, October 1977. 4 pp.

620. 605-DO "The Right to Witness!" Rome: The Children of God, October 1977. 8 pp.

621. 606-DFO "Lashes of Love!" n.p.: The Children of God, November 1977. 16 pp.

622. 607-GP "Our Declaration of Love!" Rome: The Children of God, October 1977. 3 pp.

623. 608-DFO "Say 'Goodbye' to Children!" n.p.: The Children of God, October 1977. 1 p.

624. 609-DFO "Food or Poison?!" n.p.: The Children of God, October 1977. 9 pp.

625. 610-GP "Moses on the Mountain!" n.p.: The Children of God, October 1977. 3 pp.

626. 611-DO "NNN Attack!" n.p.: The Children of God, October 1977. 4 pp.

627. —DO Mordecai. "Letter From Mordecai." n.p.: The Children of God, October 1977. 2 pp.

628. 612-DO "The Praise of Wrath!" n.p.: The Children of God, October 1977. 1 p.

629. 613-GP "Atlantis!" n.p.: The Children of God, October 1977. 2 pp.

630. 614-GP "Treasure Ship!" n.p.: The Children of God, October 1977. 7 pp.

631. 615-GP "Atlanta!—Goddess of Atlantis!" n.p.: The Children of God, October 1977. 3 pp.

632. 616-GP "'Taurug!'—The Guanche Chieftain!" n.p.: The Children of God, October 1977. 7 pp.

633. 617-DO "The Church of Love!" n.p.: The Children of God, November 1977. 7 pp.

634. 618a-DFO "His Father's Beloved!' n.p., n.d. 2 pp.

635. 618b-DFO "Elixer of Heaven (Dito Chapter 7)." n.p., n.d. 2 pp.

636. 619-DFO "Prophecy for Davidito!" n.p.: The Children of God, October 1977. 10 pp.

637. 620-GP "Holy Ghosts!" n.p.: The Children of God, November 1977. 7 pp.

638. 621-GP "More Holy Ghosts!" n.p.: The Children of God, November 1977. 7 pp.

639. 622-GP "The Spirit World!" n.p.: The Children of God, November 1977. 6 pp.

640. 623-GP "Flying Saucers!—UFO's!—Spiritual Vehicles?" n.p.: The Children of God, November 1977. 3 pp.

641. 624-GP "Spaceship!" n.p.: The Children of God, December 1977. 7 pp.

642. 625-DFO "The Tangled Lines of Hejaz!" n.p.: The Children of God, November 1977. 3 pp.

643. 626-GP "The Fan!" n.p.: The Children of God, November 1977. 3 pp.

644. 627-GP "Merlin's Hat!" n.p.: The Children of God, November 1977. 4 pp.

645. 628-GP "X-Ray Eyes!" n.p.: The Children of God, November 1977. 7 pp.

646. 629-GP "The Magic Green Shirt!" n.p.: The Children of God, November 1977. 8 pp.

647. 630-GP "Pyramid Power!" n.p.: The Children of God, December 1977. 6 pp.

648. 631-DFO "Islam—Chapter 1." n.p.: The Children of God, November 1977. 15 pp.

649.   632-DO "More on the Church of Love!" n.p.: The Children of God,
       November 1977. 7 pp.

650.   633-GP "Our Answers for the Daily News!" n.p.: The Children of God,
       November 1977. 12 pp.

651.   634-DFO "Strange Bedfellows!" n.p.: The Children of God, December
       1977. 7 pp.

652.   635-DFO "Grace vs. Law!" n.p.: The Children of God, November 1977.
       16 pp.

653.   636-DFO "Happy Birthday Jesus!" Rome: The Family of Love,
       December 1978. 4 pp.

654.   637-GP "Peace?—Or War!" n.p.: The Children of God, December 1977. 7
       pp.

655.   638-DFO Mo and Maria. "Merry Christmas!" n.p.: The Children of God,
       November 1977. 8 pp.

       Taken from item 231. (letter #194).

656.   639-DFO "Real Love Never Fails!" n.p.: The Children of God, December
       1977. 7 pp.

657.   640-GP "Mokes!" n.p.: The Children of God, December 1977. 7 pp.

658.   641-DFO "The Prodigal Son!" n.p.: The Children of God, December
       1977. 12 pp.

659.   642-GP "The Bible in Pictures!—Chapter One: The Creation and Fall Of
       Man! and Noah and the Flood!" Rome: The Children of God, September
       1977. 9 pp.

660.   643-GP "The Bible in Pictures!—Chapter 2: The Tower of Babel! and
       The Life of Abraham!" Rome: The Children of God, September 1977. 15
       pp.

661.   644-GP "The Bible in Pictures!—Chapter 3: Lot and His Wife!" and Isaac
       And Ishmael!" Rome: The Children of God, November 1977. 15 pp.

662.   645-GP "7000 Years of World History!—Part I." Rome: Mobile Schools
       Creations, 1977. 14 pp.

663.   646-DFO "A New Year's Eve Candlelight Prayer Meeting!" n.p.: The
       Children of God, December 1977. 2 pp.

664.   647-GP "Love vs. Law!" n.p.: The Children of God, January 1978. 8 pp.

665.   648-GP "Is Love Against the Law?" n.p.: The Children of God, January
       1978. 8 pp.

666.   649-DFO "Lit Laws!" n.p.: The Children of God, January 1978. 7 pp.

667. 650-DO "Re-Organization Nationalisation Revolution!" n.p.: The Children of God, January 1978. 8 pp.

668. 651-DFO "Little Nuggets!" n.p.: The Children of God, January 1978. 8 pp.

669. 652-DO "Does FF-ing Pay?" n.p.: The Children of God, January 1978. 7 pp.

670. 653-DFO "The Broken Chain!" n.p.: The Children of God, January 1978. 2 pp.

671. 654-GP "The Saddest Christmas Day?" n.p.: The Children of God?" n.p.: The Children of God, January 1978. 6 pp.

672. 655-GP "Warning!" n.p.: The Children of God, January 1978. 6 pp.

Published originally as the first GP in 1966.

673. 656-DO Mo and Maria. "Confidential Questionnaire." n.p.: The Children of God, n.d. 8 pp.

674. 657-DO "Our New Colony Rules Summarised!" n.p.: The Children of God, January 1978. 8 pp.

675. 658-DFO "'78 Here We Come!" n.p.: The Children of God, January 1978. 6 pp.

676. 659-DO "Nationalization!" n.p.: The Children of God, January 1978. 8 pp.

677. 660-DO Sarah, Mo and Maria. "The Family of Love Home Checklist." n.p.: the Family of Love, February 1978. 4 pp.

678. 661-DO Mo and Maria. "World Service Home Advisory." n.p.: The Family of Love, February 1978. 3 pp.

679. 662-DO "Where Are the Shepherds?" n.p.: The Family of Love, February 1978. 7 pp.

680. 663-DO "Happy Rebirthday!" n.p.: The Family of Love, February 1978. 5 pp.

681. 664-LTO "Cesspool!" n.p.: The Family of Love, February 1978. 4 pp.

682. 665-DO "Will Ye Also Go Away?" n.p.: The Family of Love, February 1978. 2 pp.

683. 666-DO "Alexander, the Evil Magician!" n.p.: The Family of Love, February 1978. 4 pp.

684. 667-DO "Do Ya Want the Letters or Don'tcha?" Rome: The Family of Love, February 1978. 4 pp.

685. 668-DO "Sprint Center Monthly Report.: n.p., n.d. 2 pp.

686.   669-DO Concerned, Timothy. "Pioneer Request Form." Rome: World Service, February 1978. 1 p.

687.   670R-DO Mo, Maria, W.S. and All. "Home Servants' Monthly Report Form." n.p., n.d. 4 pp.

688.   671-DO "Happy Housekeeping!" n.p.: The Family of Love, March 1978. 8 pp.

689.   672-DFO "More Lit Laws!" Rome: The Family of Love, March 1978. 4 pp.

690.   673-DFO "7 Supporters!" Rome: The Family of Love, March 1978. 7 pp.

691.   674-DO "Duties of KQS's & VS's." Rome: The Family of Love, March 1978. 8 pp.

692.   675-DO "New Brooms!" Rome: The Family of Love, March 1978. 5 pp.

693.   676-DO "The 'Dirty Dorm' Dream!" Rome: The Family of Love, March 1978. 2 pp.

694.   677-GP "The Elixir of Love!" Rome: The Family of Love, March 1978. 3 pp.

695.   678-LO "If Truth Kills, Let It Kill!" Rome: The Family of Love, March 1978. 5 pp.

696.   679-DFO "Another Holy Ghost Story!" Rome: The Family of Love, March 1978. 6 pp.

697.   680-GP "Death in Your Arms!" Rome: The Family of Love, March 1978. 8 pp.

698.   681-DO "A Prayer for the Poor!" Rome: The Family of Love, April 1978. 8 pp.

699.   682-DO "The Shepherd's Rod!" Rome: The Family of Love, April 1978. 8 pp.

700.   683-DO "Excommunication!" Rome: The Family of Love, April 1978. 7 pp.

701.   684-DO "Make It Pay!" Rome: The Family of Love, April 1978. 4 pp.

702.   685-GP "Ruth the Secret Lover!" Rome: The Family of Love, April 1978. 15 pp.

703.   686-GP "Out of This World!" Rome: The Family of Love, April 1978. 33 pp.

704.   687-DFO "Bible Reading for Children." Rome: The Family of Love, May 1978. 4 pp.

705.   688-DO "The Advantages of Having Children!" Rome: The Family of Love, May 1978. 5 pp.

706. 689-DO Maria and Timothy Concerned. "Proclaim a Fast!" n.p.: The Family of Love, 1978. 4 pp.

707. 690-GP "Daily Might No. 1." Rome: The Children of God, 1976. 8 pp.

708. 691-GP "Daily Might No. 2." n.p., 1976. 8 pp.

709. 692-GP "Daily Might No. 3." n.p.: The Family of Love, n.d. 8 pp.

710. 693-GP "7000 Years of World History!—Part II." Rome: The Family of Love, December 1978. 31 pp.

711. 694-GP "7000 Years of World History!—Part III." Rome: The Family of Love, December 1978. 23 pp.

712. 695-DFO "The Philadelphian Prophecy!" Rome: The Family of Love, May 1978. 8 pp.

713. 696-DO "Proclaim Liberty!" n.p., May 25, 1978. 3 pp.

714. 697-DO "Seek First!" Rome: The Family of Love, June 1978. 7 pp.

715. 698-DO "I Was Sick—And Ye Visited Me!" Rome: The Family of Love, June 1978. 7 pp.

716. 699-DO "You Are the Love of God!" Rome: The Family of Love, June 1978. 7 pp.

717. 700-DFO "The Operator!" Rome: The Family of Love, June 1978. 7 pp.

718. 701-DO "Own No Man!" Rome: The Family of Love, June 1978. 8 pp.

719. 702-DO "Bring Ye All the Tithe Into the Storehouse." Rome: The Family of Love, June 1978. 15 pp.

720. 703-DFO "Shtick!" Rome: The Family of Love, June 1978. 8 pp.

721. 704-DFO "Extermination!" Rome: The Family of Love, June 1978. 7 pp.

722. 705-DFO "Madame M on Maria!" Rome: The Family of Love, June 1978. 12 pp.

723. 706-DO "When I'm Gone." Rome: The Family of Love, June 1978. 5 pp.

724. 707-DO "The End-Time Witnesses!" Rome: The Family of Love, June 1978. 5 pp.

725. 708-DFO "Your 2-Year-Old Can Receive Jesus!" Rome: The Family of Love, June 1978. 9 pp.

726. 709-DFO "Islam!—Chapter 2." Rome: The Family of Love, June 1978. 6 pp.

727. 710-DFO "Close Encounter!" Rome: The Family of Love, June 1978. 7 pp.

728.   711-DFO "The Pyramid!" Rome: The Family of Love, July 1978. 3 pp.

729.   712-DFO "Hearing From God!" Rome: The Family of Love, July 1978. 2 pp.

730.   713-DFO "The Elixir!" Rome: The Family of Love, July 1978. 2 pp.

731.   714-DFO "Death?--Or Dawn!" Rome: The Family of Love, July 1978. 8 pp.

732.   715-DFO "Childcare Jewels." Rome: The Family of Love, August 1978. 6 pp.

733.   716-DO "The Division!" Rome: The Family of Love, July 1978. 8 pp.

734.   717-DFO "Expect Miracles!" Rome: The Family of Love, July 1978. 5 pp.

735.   718-DFO "The Potato!" Rome: The Family of Love, July 1978. 12 pp.

736.   719-DO "Momos!" Rome: The Family of Love, July 1978. 6 pp.

737.   720-DFO "Pity the Weak!" Rome: The Family of Love, July 1978. 6 pp.

738.   721-DO "The Girl Who Wouldn't!" Rome: The Family of Love, July 1978. 12 pp.

739.   722-DFO "The Handicapped Child--Davidito!" Rome: The Family of Love, July 1978. 11 pp.

740.   723-DFO "The Goddess of Love!" Rome: The Family of Love, 1978. 4 pp.

741.   724-DO "The Love of David!" Rome: The Family of Love, July 1978. 5 pp.

742.   725-DFO "Quote-Size Letters!" Rome: The Family of Love, July 1978. 2 pp.

743.   726-DFO "Black Holes!" Rome: The Family of Love, August 1978. 4 pp.

744.   727-DFO "Greater Victories!" Rome: The Family of Love, August 1978. 15 pp.

745.   728-DFO "Are Your Children 'Becoming One?'" Rome: The Family of Love, August 1978. 4 pp.

746.   729-DFO "Pope Paul VI Graduates!" Rome: The Family of Love, August 1978. 2 pp.

747.   730-DFO "The Dying Dollar!" Rome: The Family of Love, October 1978. 8 pp.

748.   731-DFO "New Life! New Love!—Quote Book." Rome: The Family of Love, August 1978. 20 pp.

749. 732-DFO "The Bible in Pictures!--Chapter 4: The Life of Issaac! And Jacob and Esau!" Rome: The Family of Love, September 1978. 18 pp.

750. 733-DFO "The Shah's Last Resort." Rome: The Family of Love, November 1978. 5 pp.

751. 734-LTO "Training and Shepherding Babes." Rome: The Children of God, February 1977. 15 pp.

752. 735-GP "Proof at Last!" Rome: The Children of God, September 1976. 8 pp.

753. 736-GP "Big Lie." Rome: The Children of God, September 1976. 8 pp.

754. 737-DFO "Why Are Our Children Sick? (Dito Chapter 27)." n.p., 9 October 1978. 3 pp.

755. 738-DFO "Euro-Units." Rome: The Family of Love, December 1978. 8 pp.

756. 739-DFO "Jesus Babies." Rome: The Family of Love, December 1978. 3 pp.

757. 740-DFO "Mideast Peace?" Rome: The Family of Love, November 1978. 3 pp.

758. 741-DFO "U.S. Stooges." Rome: The Family of Love, November 1978. 4 pp.

759. 742-DFO "Prophetic Interpretation of Recent World Events." Rome: The Family of Love, November 1978. 4 pp.

760. 743-GP "Love Is All You Need." n.p.: True Comix, n.d.

761. 744-DFO "God's Gift Is God's Work, Part 1." Zurich: World Services, February 1979. 7 pp.

762. 745-DFO "God's Gift Is God's Work, Part 2." Zurich: World Services, April 1979. 6 pp.

763. 746-DFO "God's Gift Is God's Work, Part 3." Rome: The Family of Love, February 1979. 7 pp.

764. 747-DFO "Happy New Year 1979!--The NRS Revolution!" Rome: The Family of Love, December 1978. 8 pp.

765. 748-DFO "What Now?! Persecution and Fleeing: NRS 2." Rome: The Family of Love, December 1978. 4 pp.

766. 749-DFO "Where to Now?: NRS 3." Rome: The Family of Love, December 1978. 4 pp.

767. 750-DFO "Going Underground: NRS 4." Rome: The Family of Love, December 1978. 4 pp.

768.   751-DFO "Homegoing II Message." n.p., 20 December 1978. 1 p.

769.   752-DFO "Why the Family?: NRS 5." Rome: The Family of Love, December 1978. 4 pp.

770.   753-DFO "Prayer for the Children." Rome: The Family of Love, January 1979. 1 p.

771.   754-GP "Dear Friend or Foe." n.p., 2 January 1979. 1 p.

772.   755-DFO Mo and Maria. "New Program for WWMM." n.p., n.d.

773.   756-DFO "Furlougher, Backslider or Supporter? NRS 6." Rome: The Family of Love, January 1978. 4 pp.

774.   757-DFO "The IRF: NRS 7." Rome: The Family of Love, January 1979. 4 pp.

775.   758-DO "Flee: NRS 8." Rome: The Family of Love, January 1979. 4 pp.

776.   759-DO "The Four Deadly Sins: NRS 9." Rome: The Family of Love, January 1979. 2 pp.

777.   760-DFO "Techi's Welcome to Spain." Zurich: World Services, February 1979. 2 pp.

778.   761-DO "Security Rules! (FN 9:11)." Rome: The Family of Love, February 1979. 3 pp.

779.   762-GP "The Crash of '79!" Zurich: World Services, February 1979. 4 pp.

780.   763-DO "The Nebuchadnezzar Revelation." Zurich: World Services, February 1979. 3 pp.

781.   764-DO "Son of Sam." Zurich: World Services, February 1979. 2 pp.

782.   765-DO "Prayer for Protection: NRS 10." Zurich: World Services, February 1979. 4 pp.

783.   766-DFO "A Job Well Done: NRS 11." Zurich: World Services, February 1979. 4 pp.

784.   767-DO "The Happy Ending: NRS 12." Zurich: World Services, February 1979. 4 pp.

785.   "Dear Mo' Ammar: an Open Letter." Zurich: World Services, March 1979. 2 pp.

786.   769-DFO "Door-to-Door Witnessing: NRS 13." n.p., 5 January 1979. 4 pp.

787.   770-DFO "The Maturation of a Movement: NRS 14." n.p., 5 January 1979. 4 pp.

788.   771-DFO "Coming of Age: NRS 15." n.p.: World Services, March 1979. 4 pp.

789. 772-DFO "Sorry Judas!--It's too Late to Quit!: NRS 16." Zurich: World Services, March 1979. 4 pp.

790. 773-DFO "Knew Disciples: Dad's Digest of World Stats." Zurich: World Services, March 1979. 4 pp.

791. 774-DFO "Hard Rock Bands." Zurich: World Services, March 1979. 1 p.

792. 775-DFO "You Are What You Read--Part 1." Zurich: World Services, May 1979. 4 pp.

793. 776-DFO "Book Burning--You Are What You Read--Part 2." Zurich: World Services, May 1979. 4 pp.

794. 777-GP "All Hail to the Queen." Zurich: World Services, April 1979. 4 pp.

795. 778-DO Dad and Maria. "Timothy's Departure." Zurich: World Services, March 1979. 4 pp.

796. 779-DO "My Childhood Sex." Zurich: World Services, May 1979. 6 pp.

797. 780-DFO "Children in the World: NRS 17." Zurich: World Services, April 1979. 6 pp.

798. 781-DO "The Lord's Supper." Zurich: World Services, May 1979. 6 pp.

799. 782-DO "Uncircumcision." Zurich: World Services, June 1979. 3 pp.

800. 783-DFO "The Exodus." n.p., n.d. 4 pp.

801. 784-DFO Paul, Marianne, Maria and David Berg. "The Timothy Revelation." Zurich: World Services, May 1979. 4 pp.

802. 785-DFO "Techi's Story Chapter 1." Zurich: World Services, May 1979. 4 pp.

803. 786-DFO "Techi's Story Chapter 2." Zurich: World Services, May 1979. 4 pp.

804. 787-DFO "Techi's Story Chapter 3. Home or Hospital?" Zurich: World Services, May 1979. 4 pp.

805. 788-DFO "Techi's Story Chapter 4." Zurich: World Services, May 1979. 4 pp.

806. 789-DFO "Techi's Story Chapter 5, Birth Miracles!" Zurich: World Services, May 1979. 3 pp.

807. 790-DFO "Techi's Story Chapter 6, Dito Meets Techi!" Zurich: World Services, May 1979. 4 pp.

808. 791-DFO "Eleven Years of Family History." Zurich: World Services, May 1979. 4 pp.

809. 792-DO "Questions from the Field—Part 1." Zurich: World Services, May 1979. 4 pp.

810. 793-DO "Questions from the Field—Part 2." Zurich: World Services, May 1979. 4 pp.

811. 794-DFO "Techi's Story Chapter 7: Where Do Babies Come From?" Zurich: World Services, May 1979. 4 pp.

812. 795-DFO "Techi's Story Chapter 8: Heavenly Techi." Zurich: World Services, May 1979. 4 pp.

813. 796-DO "The Mystery of Otano." Zurich: World Services, June 1979. 5 pp.

814. 797-DO "The Maltese Doublecross, Parts 1-4." Zurich: World Services, July 1979. 16 pp.

815. 798-DO "Boca do Inferno: Written in the Rocks." Zurich: World Services, June 1979. 2 pp.

816. 799-DFO "Prince of the Covenant, Parts 1-3." Zurich: World Services, July 1979. 13 pp.

817. 800-GP "To the Media, From a Guru, About the Cults." Zurich: World Services, June 1979. 2 pp.

818. 801-GP "Skylab and the Oil War!—'The Sky Is Falling!'" Zurich: World Services, 28 June 1979. 3 pp.

819. 802-GP "Happy Endings!—About Modern Movies and Skylab!" Zurich: World Services, 19 June 1979. 3 pp.

820. 803-DFO "In the Name of Fair Play!" n.p., July 1979. 1 p.

821. 804-DFO "Get out the Message—Money or No Money!" n.p., 5 May 1979. 1 p.

822. 805-DFO "Get Out!" n.p., 7 July 1979. 6 pp.

823. 806-DO "Go Ye!" Zurich: World Services, August 1979. 6 pp.

824. 807-DFO "Have Faith—Will Camp!—Part One." Zurich: World Services, August 1979. 40 pp.

825. 808-DO "Local Language IFR Maily Ministry for KOS's & TCC's." Zurich: World Services, 24 June 1979. 2 pp.

826. 809-DFO "Numerical ML List: 600-833.... " Zurich: World Services, October 1979. 2 pp.

827. 810-DFO "Urgent Notice!: The IRF-IRF Stat and LLIMM Revolution!" n.p., 1 August 1979. 1 p.

828. 811-DO "The Jeane Manson Revelations!" Zurich: World Services, 13 November 1977. 6 pp.

829. 812-1-DFO "Have Trailer—Will Travel!—Part 1: Fires!" Zurich: World Services, 13 July 1979. 4 pp.

830. 812-2-DFO "Have Trailer—Will Travel!—Part 2: Gas Fires!" Zurich: World Services, 13 July 1979. 4 pp.

831. 812-3-DFO "Have Trailer—Will Travel!—Part 3: Gas Fires and Campers!" Zurich: World Services, 13 July 1979. 4 pp.

832. 812-4-DFO "Have Trailer—Will Travel!—Part 4: Campers and Survival!" Zurich: World Services, 13 July 1979. 6 pp.

833. 812-5-DFO "Have Trailer—Will Travel!—Part 5: Trailers vs. Motor-Homes!" Zurich: World Services, 13 July 1979. 4 pp.

834. 812-6-DFO "Have Trailer—Will Travel!"—Part 6: Size and Weight!" Zurich: World Services. 4 pp.

835. 812-7-DFO "Have Trailer—Will Travel!—Part 7: Safety Equipment!" Zurich: World Services, 13 July 1979. 4 pp.

836. 812-8-DFO "Have Trailer—Will Travel!—Part 8: Interiors!" Zurich: World Services, 13 July 1979. 4 pp.

837. 812-9-DFO "Have Trailer—Will Travel!—Part 9: Water and Fridge!" Zurich: World Services, 13 July 1979. 4 pp.

838. 812-10-DFO "Have Trailer—Will Travel!—Part 10: Level and Stabilize!" Zurich: World Services, 13 July 1979. 4 pp.

839. 812-11-DFO "Have Trailer—Will Travel!—Part 11: Hitches!" Zurich: World Services, 13 July 1979. 4 pp.

840. 812-12-DFO "Have Trailer—Will Travel!—Part 12: Ventilation, Heat and Bathing!" n.p., 13 July 1979. 4 pp.

841. 812-13-DFO "Have Trailer—Will Travel!—Part 13: Washing!" n.p., 13 July 1979. 4 pp.

842. 812-14-DFO "Have Trailer—Will Travel!—Part 14: Toilets!" n.p., 13 July 1979. 4 pp.

843. 812-15-DFO "Have Trailer—Will Travel!—Part 15: Trailer Breakfast!" Zurich: World Services, 14 July 1979. 6 pp.

844. 812-16-DFO "Have Trailer—Will Travel!—Part 16: Pressure Cooking, Napkins and Floors!" Zurich: World Services, 14 July 1979. 5 pp.

845. 812-17-DFO "Have Trailer—Will Travel!—Part 17: Beds!" Zurich: World Services, 14 July 1979. 4 pp.

846. 812-18-DFO "Have Trailer—Will Travel!—Part 18: Windows, Curtains and Shutters." Zurich: World Services, 14 July 1979. 3 pp.

847. 812-19-DFO "Have Trailer—Will Travel!—Part 19: Lights, Ventilation, Hook-Ups, Camps!" Zurich: World Services, 14 July 1979. 10 pp.

848. 812-20-DFO "Have Trailer—Will Travel!—Part 20: Trailer Driving!" Zurich: World Services, 14 July 1979. 10 pp.

849. 812-21-DFO "Have Trailer—Will Travel!—Part 21: Roadside Repairs!" Zurich: World Services, 14 July 1979. 8 pp.

850. 812-22-DFO "Have Trailer—Will Travel!—Part 22: Freezing!" Zurich: World Services, 21 December 1979. 8 pp.

851. 812-23-DFO "Have Trailer—Will Travel!—Part 23: Parking, Telephones and Radios!" Zurich: World Services, 14 July 1979. 7 pp.

852. 812-24-DFO "Trailer Lights!—How to Hook'm Up!" Zurich: World Services, 9 May 1980. 4 pp.

853. 813-DFO "Prayer of a Good Shepherd!" n.p., 2 December 1978. 3 pp.

854. 814-DFO "No Lit?—No Letters!" Zurich: World Services, 13 August 1979. 4 pp.

855. 815-GP David, Father and Sara Davidito. "Sex Questions and Answers! Part 1." Zurich: World Services, September 1979. 7 pp.

856. 816-GP David, Father and Maria. "Sex Questions and Answers. Part 2." Zurich: World Services, September 1979. 7 pp.

857. 616-2-GP "Sex Questions and Answers!—Part Three." Zurich: Family Services, March 1980. 4 pp.

858. 817-DO "FF Questions and Answers." n.p., December 1978. 6 pp.

859. 818-GP "Sex in Heaven!" Zurich: World Services, July 1970. 6 pp.

860. 819-DO "Dad's Prayer for the 'RNR'!" n.p., 14 February 1978. 4 pp.

861. 820-DO "More on the Spirit of God!" n.p., 20 September 1978. 1 p.

862. 821-DO "A Letter from Dad to the Pacific's former leaders!" n.p., 16 February 1978. 2 pp.

863. 822-GP "Daily Might No. 4." n.p., 1979.

864. 823-GP "Daily Might No. 5." n.p., September 1979.

865. 824-GP "Daily Might No. 6." n.p., September 1979.

866. 825-GP "Daily Might No. 7." n.p., October 1979.

867. 826-GP "Daily Might No. 8." n.p., October 1979.

868. 827-DFO David, Maria. "Techi's Story!—Chapter 9: Recovery." n.p., 9 August 1979. 6 pp.

869. 828-DO "The RFN Dream!" Zurich: World Services, 25 May 1979. 4 pp.

870. 829-GP "7 Ways to Know God's Will!" Zurich: World Services, Summer 1968. 5 pp.

871. 830-DFO "Handicapped?" Zurich: World Services, May 1979. 4 pp.

872. 831-1-DFO "'Motion Sickness!'—Chapter 1: It's Subconscious Fear!" Zurich: World Services, 12 May 1977. 3 pp.

873. 831-2-DFO "'Motion Sickness!'—Chapter 2: It's Psychosomatic!" Zurich: World Services, 12 May 1977. 4 pp.

874. 831-3-DFO "'Motion Sickness!'—Chapter 3: How to Control It!" Zurich: World Services, 12 May 1977. 4 pp.

875. 831-4-DFO "'Motion Sickness!'—Chapter 4: It's Mind Over Matter!" Zurich: World Services, 12 May 1977. 4 pp.

876. 832-DO "The KQL Revolution!" Zurich: World Services, 10 September 1979. 4 pp.

877. 833-DFO "The Latest News!" Zurich: World Services, October 1979. 6 pp.

878. 834-DFO "It's Time to Invade the Churches!" Zurich: World Services, 21 September 1979. 1 p.

879. 835-1-DFO "Frustrated?—Part I." Zurich: World Services, 22 September 1979. 4 pp

880. 835-2-DFO "Frustrated?—Part II." Zurich: World Services, 22 September 1979. 4 pp.

881. 835-3-DFO "Frustrated?—Part III." Zurich: World Services, 22 September 1979. 4 pp.

882. 835-4-DFO "Frustrated?—Part IV." n.p., 22 September 1979. 4 pp.

883. 836a-DFO "Dirty Homes!" Zurich: World Services, 23 September 1979. 6 pp.

884. 836b-DO "Sequel to 'Dirty Homes!'" n.p., October 1979. 4 pp.

885. 837-DO "The Shepherdess!" Zurich: World Services, 25 September 1979. 8 pp.

886. 838-DFO "The Unguarded Moment!" Zurich: World Services, 29 November 1979. 2 pp.

887. 839-DO "The Wounds of a Friend!" Zurich: World Services, August 1979. 2 pp.

888. 840-DO "The Trouble with the System Is: Problems!" Zurich: World Services, October 1979. 2 pp.

889. 841-DO "The Family Aid Fund!" Zurich: World Services, October 1979. 2 pp.

890.   842-1-DFO "Good News for Bilingual Homes!" n.p., 20 October 1979. 2 pp.

891.   842-2-DO "Dear KQL's, CRO's and LLIMM's—Bilingual Homes Procedures: Part 2." n.p., 30 October 1979. 2 pp.

892.   843-DO "No More Do's for Only $20!" Zurich: World Services, 31 October 1979. 7 pp.

893.   844-DFO "Artists' Advisory No. 6." Zurich: World Services, October 1979. 4 pp.

894.   845-DO "The Secret!" Zurich: World Services, 13 April 1978. 4 pp.

895.   846-DFO "Autumn '79 Investment Seminar!" Zurich: World Services, 7 October 1979. 2 pp.

896.   847-DO "The King's Love!" Zurich: World Services, 15 April 1978. 6 pp.

897.   848-1-DFO "The Sinking Truck!: The Church Ministry!" Zurich: World Services, 18 October 1979. 5 pp.

898.   848-2-DFO "The Sinking Truck!" the Dangers of Going to Church!" n.p., 18 October 1979. 23 pp.

899.   848-3-DFO "The Sinking Truck!: The Mobile Ministry!" n.p., 18 October 1979. 29 pp.

900.   849-DO "Sergeant York!" n.p., 15 April 1978. 4 pp.

901.   850-1-DFO "Life After Death!—Part 1." n.p., 19 June 1978. 6 pp.

902.   850-2-DFO "Life After Death!—Part 2." n.p., 19 June 1978. 5 pp.

903.   851-1-DFO "What Every Driver Should Know!—Chapter 1: Brakes and Bearings." Zurich: World Services, 10 July 1979. 4 pp.

904.   851-2-DFO "What Every Driver Should Know!—Chapter 2: Oil, Water and Tire Pressure." Zurich: World Services, 10 July 1979. 4 pp.

905.   851-3-DFO "What Every Driver Should Know!—Chapter 3: The Daily Check!" Zurich: World Services, 10 July 1979. 4 pp.

906.   851-4-DFO "What Every Driver Should Know!—Chapter 4: Time for a Tune-Up!" Zurich: World Services, 10 July 1979. 6 pp.

907.   851-5-DFO "What Every Driver Should Know!—Chapter Five: The Overhaul." Zurich: World Services, 10 July 1979. 6 pp.

908.   851-6-DFO "What Every Driver Should Know!—Chapter Six: Battery Care and Starting!" Zurich: World Services, 3 December 1979. 11 pp.

909.   852-GP "When Morning Dawns!" Zurich: World Services, September 1979. 12 pp.

910. 853-DO "An Answer to BBC!" n.p., 4 December 1979. 1 p.

911. 854-DFO "The Crash Is Here!" n.p., 5 January 1980. 2 pp.

912. 855-DFO "Emergency Tidbits!" n.p., 14 January 1980. 2 pp.

913. 856-DO "The Christmas Eve Massacre!" n.p., 25 December 1979. 10 pp.

914. 857-DO "Terror by Night!" Zurich: World Services, 10 January 1980. 4 pp.

915. 858-DFO "Be Prepared!" Zurich: World Services, January 1980. 8 pp.

916. 859-DFO "Survival for Families!" n.p., January 1980. 7 pp.

917. 860-DO Provisioner, Emmanuel, Meggido French, Gideon Valor, Elias Burnfree and Dad. "Provisioning!" n.p., January 1980. 9 pp.

918. 861-1-DFO Valor, Gideon. "Tents and Sleeping Bags!--Part One: Tents." n.p., January 1980. 2 pp.

919. 861-2-DFO Valor, Gideon. "Tents and Sleeping Bags!--Pat Two: Sleeping Bags." n.p., January 1980. 2 pp.

920. 862-DFO "To Whom Shall We Go?" n.p., 18 January 1980. 1 p.

921. 863-DFO David, Maria. "Techi's Story!--Chapter 10: Breastfeeding!" Zurich: World Services, August 1979. 12 pp.

922. 864-DFO David, Maria. "Techi's Story!--Chapter 11: Convalescence." Zurich: World Services, August 1979. 3 pp.

923. 865-DO "Apocalypse Now!" Zurich: World Services, 1 January 1980. 6 pp.

924. 866-DO "Emergency Notice: 'Owe No Man!'—Part 2." Zurich: World Services, 26 January 1980. 2 pp.

925. 867-DO Valor, Gideon. "Why the Crash?" Zurich: World Services, January 1980. 10 pp.

926. 868-DFO "Happy Birthday, Dear Family!" n.p., 27 January 1980. 1 p.

927. 869-DO "The War Has Begun!" Zurich: World Services, 5 February 1980. 7 pp.

928. 870-DFO "Mo-bility!" n.p., n.d. 2 pp.

929. 871-DFO Mo and Maria. "Warning Notice! (Re: LIM's)." n.p., n.d. 1 p.

930. 871-A-DO "LIT-PIC Notice!" n.p., 10 March 1980. 1 p.

931. 872-DO "'Road Mail' Notice!—How to Get Your Mail Though on The Road!" n.p., 11 February 1980. 6 pp.

932.   873-DFO "Dad's Comments on the Komix!" n.p., n.d. 2 pp.

933.   874-DO "The Mrs. Mugabe Nightmare!" Zurich: World Services, 3 February 1980. 3 pp.

934.   875-DO "The Black Nightmare!" Zurich: World Services, 3 February 1980. 6 pp.

935.   876-DO "No More Free Sealed Mailings!" n.p., 13 February 1980. 1 p.

936.   877-DO "Dad's Birthday Message!" Zurich: World Services, 18 February 1980. 17 pp.

937.   878-DFO "Fevers!—The 'Poisonous Plum' and Tonsilitis!" Zurich: World Services, 11 July 1979. 4 pp.

938.   879-DO "The Ronald Reagan Spider Dream!" Zurich: World Services, 5 March 1980. 4 pp.

939.   880-DFO "IRFERS Beware!" Zurich: World Services, February 1980. 8 pp.

940.   881-DO "Hustler Reprint." n.p., n.d. 1 p.

941.   882-DFO "New Models!" Zurich: World Services, 25 March 1979. 15 pp.

942.   883-DO "The Nuke Game!—Or 'The Push Button War'!" Zurich: World Services, 5 March 1980. 2 pp.

943.   884-DO Virginia. "Grandma's Letter About Baby David!" Zurich: World Services, April 1980. 2 pp.

944.   885-DO "Emergency Funds!" Zurich: World Services, 7 April 1980. 2 pp.

945.   886-DFO "Late Report, No Mag!" Zurich: World Services, 4 April 1980. 1 p.

946.   887-DFO "No Mo' MO FO' DFO!" Zurich: World Services, 10 April 1980. 2 pp.

947.   888-DO "Emergency Notice to TRFers Only: No Mo' Blank TRFS!" n.p., 10 April 1980. 1 p.

948.   889-DFO "No Mo' MO Thieves, Robbers, Bootleggers, and Black Marketeers!" n.p., 10 April 1980. 2 pp.

949.   890-DO "Media Crucifixion!" n.p., 15 March 1980. 1 p.

950.   891-DFO "Nightmare in California!" n.p., 12 March 1980. 1 p.

951.   892-DFO "Free Books!" Zurich: World Services, 8 April 1980. 2 pp.

952.   893-DO "Gold Coins!" n.p., 16 March 1980. 2 pp.

953.   894-DFO "The Electric Angel!—And Three Gold Coins!" Zurich: World Services, 11 April 1980. 4 pp.

954. 895-DO "Warning to Mailbox Litnessers!" n.p., n.d. 1 p.

955. 896-DFO "Lost Mail Report!" n.p. 1 p.

956. 897-DO "Millions of Miles of Miracles!" Zurich: World Services, 29 December 1979. 76 pp.

957. 898-DO "Africa Reverts to Savagery!" Zurich: World Services, 9 March 1980. 7 pp.

958. 899-GP "Refuge From the Storm!" Zurich: World Services, 9 March 1980. 7 pp.

959. 900-DO "He'll Care for His Own!" Zurich: World Services, 28 March 1980. 4 pp.

960. T-GP "More on Faith!" Rome: The Children of God, July 1969. 10 pp.

961. U-DO "A Parable of David and Saul." Rome: The Children of God, Summer 1970. 5 pp.

B. ALPHABETICAL LISTING

The following items are the same as those cited in the preceding section. They are listed once again, alphabetically, as an aid to cross referencing. The numbers at the end of the citations refer to the letter numbers themselves, not the item numbering.

* "Aaron on the Mountain" #234.

* "Abrahim—How Arabs Became Gypsies!" #301

* "Abrahim—The Gypsy King!" #296

* "Abrahim—'The Gypsy Story'" #298

* "Administration Revolution, The" #357

* "Advantages of Having Children, The" #688

* "Adventures of a Flirty Fish!, The" #532

* "Advice on Publications" #156B

* "Advice on 10:36'ers" #91

* "Afflictions!" #569

* "Africa Reverting to Savagery!" #898

* "African Nightmare, The" #201

* "After the Louisiana Festival of Life" #97

* "Aladdin's Lamp—Gaddafi's Magic?" #226

* "Alexander the Evil Magician!" #666

* "Alice and the Magic Garden" #290

* "All Hail to the Queen" #777

* "All Things Change, but Jesus Never!" #6

* "All Things Tree" #302A

* "Almond Tree, The" #158

* "Amanuensis" # 335B

* "America the Whore" #216

* "American Holocaust, The" #372

* "Amerikan Way, The" #214A

* "An Answer to BBC!" #853

* "Angola Dream, The" #390

* "Another Holy Ghost Story!" #679

* "Antenna, The" #307B

* "Anti-'God War', The" #257 and #585R

* "Apocalypse Now!" #865

* "Arab Wall, The" #274

* "Are the Children of God a Sect?" #179

* "Are We Catholics of Protestants?" #184

* "Are You a Good Sport?" #179A

* "Are You a Sight-Seer, or a Seer-Sighter?" #7

* "Are Your Children Becoming One?" #728

* "Aries—The Ram" #302B

* "Arrivederci Roma!" #180

* "Art Advisory No. 6" #844

* "Art of Oh!, The" #236

* "Ask Any Communist" #256

* "Asylum, The" #221

* "Atlanta!" #615

* "Atlantis!" #613

* "Attack!" # 171

* "August '79 Investment Seminar!" # 846

* "Baalzebub—Lord of the Flies" #168

* "Baby, The" #213

* "Baby the Babes Prophecy" #18

* "Backsliders" #140

* "Backsliding" #313C

* "Bait That Fell in Love with a Fish, The" #552

* "Battle for Africa, The" #391

* "Battle for Katanga and Famagusta!, The" #574

* "Beauty and the Beasts" #309

* "Beauty for Ashes" #114

* "Becky's Nights! (K.A.N. Ch. 9)" #507

* "Becky's Own Story! (K.A.N. Ch. 10)" #508

* "Become One" #208

* "Bell, Book and Candle" #203

* "Benefits of Backsliding, The" #312

* "Be Prepared!" #858

* "Be So Happy!" #159

* "Bewitched!" #291

* "Bible in Pictures!, The (Ch. 1)" #642

* "Bible in Pictures!, The (Ch. 2)" #643

* "Bible in Pictures!, The (Ch. 3)" #644

* "Bible in Pictures!: Isaac, Jacob and Esau" #732

* "Bible Reading for Children" #687

* "Bible Study" #96

* "Big Fish Becomes the Big Fisherman, The" #521

* "Big Lie (MO-ED)" #736

* "Birds and the Seeds, The" #316A

* "Black Holes" #726

* "Black Nightmare!, The" #875

* "Blob Story, The" #316B

* "Blob War, The (MWWFL No. 21)" #315B

* "Bloodless Coup, The" #329A

* "Bloodsuckers, The" #374

* "Boat Travel" #337C

* "Boat Trip and Hannah" #5

* "Boca Do Inferno: Written in the Rocks" #798

* "Bomb Dreams, The" #378

* "Book Burning—You Are What You Read, Part 2" #776

* "Border Bases" #178

* "Brave Pioneers" #209

* "Breakdown" #66

* "British in Uganda and Strategy in Lebanon, The" #523

* "Broken Chain!, The" #653

* "Brother Sun" #225

* "Brunheld" #326C

* "Builders Beware!" #309B

* "Burn Free!" #O

* "But if Not ...!" #313

* "Bye Bye Birdie!" #231

* "Bye Bye Miss American Pie!" #232

* "Call of David, The" #79

* "Call of India" #177

* "Casting out Demons" #K

* "Catch!, The" #555

* "Cesspool!, The" #664

* "Challenge of Godahfi" #342

* "Change the World!" #565

* "Childcare Jewels" #715

* "Cost of Flirty Fishing! (K.A.N. Ch. 2), The" #501

* "Crash, The" #284

* "Crash Is Here!, The" #854

* "Crash of '79, The" #762

* "Credits, Designations, Sharing and Rewards" #317A

* "Cromwell" #65

* "Crystal Pyramid, The" #214

* "Crystal Stream, The" #361

* "Current Events" #149

* "Dad's Birthday Message!" #877

* "Dad's Comments on the Komix!" #873

* "Dad's Prayer for the RNR! (FN2:2)" #819

* "Daily Might No. 1" #690

* "Daily Might No. 2" #691

* "Daily Might No. 3" #692

* "Daily Might No. 4" #822

* "Daily Might No. 5" #823

* "Daily Might No. 6" #824

* "Daily Might No. 7" #825

* "Daily Might No. 8" #826

* "Dancer, The" #323

* "Daniel 2" #343

* "Daniel 7" #346

* "Daniel 8" #347

* "Daniel 9" #348

* "Daniel 10, 11 and 12" #349

* "Dark Kingdom, The" #365

* "David" #77

*   "Does FF-ing Pay?" #652

*   "Dollar, The" #103

*   "Don Quixote" #198

*   "Don't Drop Out!—Drom In!" #542

*   "Door-To-Door Witnessing (NRS 13)" #769

*   "Doubts!" #604

*   "Do You Want the Letters or Don'tcha?!" #667

*   "Draft, The" #121

*   "Dreams of England" #13

*   "Dreams of Jeremiah 40" #163

*   "Drop-Outs! (Part I)" #42

*   "Drop-Outs! (Part IV)" #34

*   "Drugstore, The" #266

*   "Duggar Academy" #119

*   "Dumps" #33

*   "Duties of the KQS'S and the VS's" #674

*   "Dying Dollar, The" #730

*   "Early Church, The" #331

*   "Economy Revolution, The" #330A

*   "Education Revolution, The" #371

*   "802 South" #187

*   "Electric Angel!, The" #894

*   "Eleven Years of Family History" #791

*   "Elixir, The" #713

*   "Elixir of Love!, The" #677

*   "Elixirs of Heaven!" #618

*   "Emergency!, The" #160A

*   "Emergency Call Home" #144A

* "Emergency Funds!" #885

* "Emergency Notice: 'Owe No Man!'" #866

* "Emergency Tidbits!" #855

* "Empty Wind, The" #367

* "End of Allende, The" #272

* "Endtime Whispering Vision, The" #334

* "End-time Witnesses, The" #707

* "Epistle to a Leader" #39

* "Epistle to Pastors I" #47

* "Epistle to Pastors II (Romans Ch. 1)" #48

* "Epistle to Pastor III" #49

* "Eritrea!" #333B

* "Europa" #282

* "Euro-Units" #738

* "Evil Horse!, The" #578

* "Excommunication!" #683

* "Exodus, The" #783

* "Exorcism" #303

* "Expect Miracles" #717

* "Explosion!" #334B

* "Explosions I" #69

* "Explosions II" #69A

* "Extermination" #704

* "Fair Sex!" #326B

* "Faith" #73

* "Faith and Healing" #M

* "Faith's Lost Sheep Prophecies" #154A

* "Family Aid Fund, The" #841

* "Family of Love Home Checklist" #660

* "Family of Love!, The —The Children of God?--Mortal Sin or Salvation?" #502R

* "Family News (MWWFL No. 25)" #318C

* "Fan!, The" #626

* "Feedin' the Fish!" #543

* "Feed My Sheep!" #233

* "Feet of Faith" #87

* "Fevers!" #878

* "FF Behavior!" #563

* "FF Coupling!" #562

* "FFer's Handbook!, The" #559

* "FF Explosion!, The" #576

* "F-Fing!" #527

* "FFing and Jealousy!" #603

* "FF Questions" #817

* "FF Revolution!, The" #575

* "FF Tips!" #548

* "51 Errors of 'Daily Notices'!, The" #591

* "Fighters!" #551

* "Fishing Fever!" #550

* "Flatlanders (Organization III)" #57

* "Flee (NRS 8)" #758

* "Flee as a Bird!" #160B

* "Flee the City!" #379

* "Flesh or Spirit" #45

* "Flood, The" #220

* "Flying Saucers!—UFOs!—Spiritual Vehicles?" #623

* "Follow God! (Tape 3)" #4

*   "Food or Poison?" #609

*   "Forsaking All" #314A

*   "40 Days" #280

*   "Four Deadly Sins, The (NRS 9)" #759

*   "Four Dreams of New Colonies" #26

*   "Four Fishing Failures" #533

*   "France Our Friend (MWWFL No. 14)" #313B

*   "Free Books!" #892

*   "Freed! (K.A.N. Ch. 15)" #513

*   "French Connection, The" #335C

*   "Fret Not!" #317B

*   "Frog, The" #275

*   "'From Whence Come Wars?'" #601

*   "Frozen Book, The" #383

*   "Frustrated, Part I" #835-1

*   "Frustrated, Part II" #835-2

*   "Frustrated, Part III" #835-3

*   "Frustrated, Part IV" #835-4

*   "Furlougher, Backslider or Supporter?" #756

*   "Gaddafi and the Children of God!" #246

*   "Gaddafi's March" #247

*   "Gaddafi's Third World" #245

*   "General Epistle to Leaders" #24

*   "George" #36

*   "Get It Together" #123

*   "Get Out!" #805

*   "Get out the Message!"

*   "Getting Organized" #297

* "Girl Who Wouldn't, The" #721

* "Glamour or Glory?" #328

* "Goddess of Love, The" #723

* "Goddesses, The" #224

* "God's Bosoms!" #581

* "God's Eyes" #544

* "God's Gift Is God's Work—Part I" #744

* "God's Gift Is God's Work—Part II" #745

* "God's Gift Is God's Work—Part III" #746

* "God's Little Miracles Part I (Tape 1)" #1

* "God's Little Miracles Part II (Tape 2)" #2

* "God's Love Slave!" #537

* "God's Only Law Is Love!" #592

* "God's Whores!" #560

* "God's Witches!" #573

* "Going Underground (NRS 4)" #750

* "Golden Seeds" #254

* "Good News for Bilingual Homes!" #842

* "Good Sample, A" #50

* "Gotcher 'Flee Gag'?" #386

* "Go Ye!" #806

* "Grace vs. Law!" #635

* "Grandma's Letter about Baby David!" #884

* "Grandmother and the Flood" #375

* "Great Escape!, The" #160

* "Greater Victories" #727

* "Green Door, The" #262

* "Green Paper Pig, The" #243

* "Greeting (From Good Sample)" #50A

* "Gypsies, The" #61

* "Halloween Wheel, The" #363

* "Hamburger Boat, The" #340

* "Handicapped?" #830

* "Handicapped Child, The" #722

* "Happy Birthday, Dear Family!" #868

* "Happy Birthday Jesus!" #636

* "Happy Ending, The (NRS 12)" #767

* "Happy Endings!—About Modern Movies!" #802

* "Happy Housekeeping!" #671

* "Happy New 1976!" #382

* "Happy New Year 1979 (The NRS Revolution)" #747

* "Happy New Year! (MWWFL No. 26)" #322A

* "Happy Rebirthday!" #663

* "Hard Rock Bands" #774

* "Have Faith—Will Camp!—Part One" #807-1

* "Have Faith—Will Camp!--Part 4—A Happy Healthy Life!" #807-4

* "Have Faith—Will Camp!—Part 6—Car-Camping and Tent Trailers!" #807-6

* "Have Faith—Will Camp!--Part 3—Food, Travel Light, Outdoors!" #807-3

* "Have Faith--Will Camp!--Part 5—Freedom, Guns and Wild Food!" #807-5

* "Have Faith—Will Camp!—Part 7—Stoves, Lanterns and Picnic Tables!" #807-7

* "Have Faith—Will Camp!--Part 8--Stoves, Tables and Dishes, Swimming!" #807-8

* "Have Faith—Will Camp!—Part 10—Tents and Cots vs. Air Mattresses!" #807-10

* "Have Faith—Will Camp!--Part 2—Utensils, Provisioning and Food" #807-2

* "Hearing From God" #712

* "Heavenly Conversation" #93

* "Heavenly Homes" #316

* "Heavenly Visitor, A (Abner)" #72

* "Heidi" #206

* "He Is Not a Jew Prophecy" #8

* "He stands in the Gap!" #73A

* "He Tells His Own Story (K.A.N. Ch. 6)" #504

* "He'll Care for His Own!" #900

* "Hitch Your Wagon to a Star! (MWWFL No. 5)" #311B

* "Holy Ghosts" #620

* "Holy Holes!" #237

* "Holy War, The" #335A

* "Homegoing, The" #145

* "Homegoing II Message" #751

* "Home Servants' Monthly Report Form" #670

* "Homos" #719

* "Hooked! (K.A.N. Ch. 13)" #511

* "Hooker!, The (K.A.N. Ch. 7)" #505

* "Howard Hughes" #199

* "How To!" #331B

* "How to Charm a Fish with a Flame! (K.A.N. Ch. 5)" #503

* "How to Close Up a Colony (Footnote to Persecution)" #125A

* "How to Survive in a Small Colony" #326C

* "How to Survive War" #311

* "How to Take It!" #597

* "100-Fold!" #881

* "Hypnotized! (K.A.N. Ch. 11)" #509

* "Jesus People—Or Revolution?" #148

* "Jewels Galore!" #539

* "Jimmy Carter" #520

* "Job Well Done, A (NRS 11)" #766

* "Judas" #71

* "Kennedy" #288

* "Key of David, The" #78

* "King Arthur's Knight! (K.A.N. Ch. 21)" #519

* "Kingdom, The" #185

* "Kingdom Prophecies—Glories of the Future!" #94

* "King Meets King! (K.A.N. Ch. 3)" #502

* "Kings" #212

* "King's Love!, The" #847

* "Knew Disciples: Dad's Digest of World Stats" #773

* "Know the Share!" #316C

* "KQL Revolution!, The" #832

* "Labour Leaders" #161

* "Lady Luck!" #602

* "Land of Not Too Much, The" #396

* "Lashes of Love!" #606

* "Last American Nightmare?, The" #381

* "Last Ranch Prophecy" #R

* "Late News!" #596

* "Late Report, No Mag!" #886

* "Latest News!" #833

* "Law of Love, The" #302C

* "Laws of Moses, The" #155

* "Let My People Go!" #144

* "Let's Talk About Jesus!" #20

* "Letters I" #51

* "Letters II" #52

* "Letters III" #53

* "Letters IV" #55

* "Letter to a Labourer" #325

* "Letter to a Loved One" #G

* "Letter to a Lover!" #526

* "Letter to America" #385

* "Letter to the Office Team" #22

* "Let the Dead Bury the Dead!" #153

* "Life After Death! Parts 1 and 2" #850

* "Listening?--Or Lamenting?" #320

* "Lit Laws!" #649

* "LIT-PIC Notice!" #871A

* "Lit Revolution, The" #328A

* "Little Book and the Time of the Gentiles, The" #146

* "Little Dog Dream, The" #535

* "Little Flirty Fishy, The" #293

* "Little Jewels!" #530

* "Little Nuggets!" #651

* "LLIMM (Local Language IRF Mail Ministry)" #808

* "Local Pubs" #318B

* "London" #58

* "Looking Unto Jesus" #126

* "Look of Love" #304

* "Lord Byron's Surrender" #301C

* "Lord's Supper, The" #781

* "Lost Mail Report" #896

* "Love Is All You Need (Comic)" #743

* "Lovelight!" #307

* "Love-Making in the Spirit" #P

* "Love Never Fails!" #25

* "Love of David, The" #724

* "Lovest Thou Me? (MWWFL No. 4)" #311A

* "Love vs. Law!" #647

* "Madame M" #268

* "Madame M on Maria" #705

* "Maharishi of Hyderabad, The" #202

* "Magic Green Shirt!, The" #629

* "Makarios" #230

* "Make It Pay!" #684

* "Male or Female?" #529

* "Maltese Doublecross, The: Parts 1-4" #797

* "Maria's Nights! (K.A.N. Ch. 8)" #506

* "Marriage Problems (MWWFL No. 15)" #314B

* "Maryknoll Fathers, The" #200

* "Maturation of a Movement, The (NRS 14)" #770

* "Media Crucifixion!" #890

* "Meek, The" #205

* "Mene, Mene, Tekel, Upharsin" #162

* "Men Who Play God!, The" #564

* "Merlin's Hat!" #627

* "Merry Christmas!" #638

* "Mideast Peace?" #740

* "Millions of Miles of Miracles!" #897

* "Ministry of Love!" #538

* "Ministry of the Mail" #51A

* "Missionary's Prayer, A" #556

* "MO-bility!" #870

* "Mocumba!" #554

* "Mokes!" #640

* "MO Letter Index Volume I" #267

* "MO Letter Index Volume II" #300

* "MO Letter Index Volume III" #320A

* "MO Letter Reprinting List, The" #229

* "Mo' Li'l Jewels!" #536

* "MO Meets Mo'amar Godahfi!" #394

* "Money Explodes, The" #294

* "Monster, The" #175

* "Monster on the Move, The" #176

* "MO on America!" #558

* "More Holy Ghosts!" #621

* "More Lit Laws!" #672

* "More on Faith" #U

* "More on Feedin' the Fish!" #549

* "More on Gaddafi!" #248

* "More on 'How To'!" #331C

* "More on Kohoutek" #278

* "More on Solaris" #271B

* "More on the Church of Love!" #632

* "More on the Spirit of God (FN 7:1)" #820

* "More Precious Pearls!" #540

* "More Prophecies on Old and New Church" #117

* "More Truth!" #598

* "More U.S. Nightmares!" #380

* "More War" #289

* "Morning Prayer" #98

* "Moses on the Mountain!" #610

* "MO's Music!" #399

* "MO's Newsletter and Advisory" #189

* "MO's Pointers for Health (The Health Revolution)" #353

* "MO Song Tapes—I and II" #95

* "MO's Worldwide Family Letter No. 1" #310A

* "MO's Worldwide Family Letter No. 2" #310B

* "MWWFL No. 4 (Lovest Thou Me?)" #311A

* "MWWFL No. 5 (Hitch Your Wagon to a Star!)" #311B

* "MWWFL Nos. 6, 7 and 8" #311C

* "MWWFL No. 9 (Paris Piss Off!)" #312A

* "MWWFL Nos. 10, 11 and 12" #312B

* "MWWFL No. 13" #312C

* "MWWFL No. 14 (France Our Friend)" #313B

* "MWWFL No. 15 (Marriage Problems)" #314B

* "MWWFL Nos. 16, 17 and 18" #314C

* "MWWFL Nos. 19 and 20 (Telephone Traitors and Problem Pastors)" #315A

* "MWWFL No. 21 (The Blob War)" #315B

* "MWWFL No. 22 (Indigenous)" #315C

* "MWWFL No. 23" #317C

* "MWWFL No. 24 (Local Pubs!)" #318B

* "MWWFL No. 25 (Family News)" #318C

* "MWWFL No. 26 (Happy New Year!)" #322A

* "Mothers of God!, The" #572

* "Motion Sickness: How to Control It!" #831-3

* "Motion Sickness: Mind Over Matter!" #831-4

* "Motion Sickness: Psychosomatic!" #831-2

* "Motion Sickness: Subconscious Fear!" #831-1

* "Mountain Island Villa Dream" #21

* "Mountain Island Villa Found" #63

* "Mountain Men" #B

* "Mountainslide" #120

* "Mountain' Maid!" #240

* "Mrs. Mugabe Nightmare!, The" #874

* "Musical Key" #326

* "Music That Made the Revolution, The" #166

* "My Childhood Sex" #779

* "My Love Is a Legend" #84

* "My Love Is the Wild Wind" #154B

* "My Love Letter—to You!" #584

* "Mystery of Otano, The" # 796

* "My Yoke Is Easy" #169

* "Name of Jesus!, The" #345

* "Naming the Baby!" #338

* "Nationalization!" #659

* "Nebuchadnezzar Revelation, The" #763

* "Nehemiah (Persecution)" #D

* "New Appointments" #377

* "New Bottles" #251

* "New Brooms!" #675

* "New Colonies" #59

* "New Colonies II" #60

* "New Leadership Revolution, The" #329C

* "New Life! (K.A.N. Ch. 20)" #518

* "New Life! New Love!--Quote Book (MO-ED)" #731

* "New Models!" #882

* "New Nation Prophecy (Personal Answers)" #64

* "New Program for WWMM" #755

* "Newsletter and Advisory No. 2" #190

* "New Teams" #62

* "New Years's Eve Candlelight Prayer Meeting, A" #646

* "Night Crawlers!, The (K.A.N. Ch. 1)" #501

* "Nightmare in California!" #891

* "99 Theses" #174

* "Nitler" #108

* "NNN Attack!" #611

* "No Lit?--No Letters!" #814

* "No Mo' Blank TRFs!" #888

* "No Mo' MO Thieves and Robbers ...!" #889

* "No Mo' MO Fo' DFO!" #887

* "No More DOs for Only #20!" #843

* "No More Free Sealed Mailings!" #876

* "Nuke Game!, The" #883

* "Numerical ML List: 600-833" #809

* "Nuns of Love!" #570

* "Odd Couple!, The (K.A.N. Ch. 4)" #502

* "Odd Couple Return!, The (K.A.N. Ch. 23)" #522

* "Office of a Bishop" #210

* "Oh of Art!, The" #325A

* "Old Bottles" #242

* "Old Church, New Church Prophecy" #A

* "Old Phonograph, The" #362

* "One Man--One Vote" #10

* "One That Got Away!, The (Part I)" #524

* "One That Got Away!, The (Part II)" #525

* "One Way (From Israel)" #86

* "One Wife" #249

* "Open Letter to Our Friends, An" #193

* "Open the Door for the Children!" #588

* "Operation P.A.C.C." #164

* "Operator!, The" #700

* "Oplexicon" #260

* "Ordination" #337A

* "Organization" #54

* "Organization II" #56

* "Other Sheep" #167

* "Our Answers!" #589

* "Our Answers to the Daily News!" #633

* "Our Declaration of Love!" #607

* "Our Family Symbol" #600

* "Our Message" #330

* "Our New Colony Rules Summarized!" #657

* "Our Replies!" #590

* "Our Report to 'Time'" #593

* "Our Shepherd, Moses David" #351

* "Out of This World!" #686

* "Owe No Man" #701

* "Poison in Paradise" #366

* "Political System, The" #333

* "Pope Paul VI Graduates (FN 5:8)" #729

* "Potato, The" #718

* "Praise of Wrath!, The" #612

* "Prayer" #369

* "Prayer for a Queen" #181

* "Prayer for Love and Mercy" #75

* "Prayer for Protection (NRS 10)" #765

* "Prayer for the Children" #753

* "Prayer for the Poor!, A" #681

* "Prayer for the Prime Minister" #186

* "Prayer in the Spirit" #252

* "Prayer of a Good Shepherd! (FN 13:3)" #813

* "Prayer of Intercession" #81

* "Prayer Power" #302

* "Priestesses of Love!, The" #561

* "Prince of the Covenant, Parts 1-3" #799

* "Problem Kings" #217

* "Problems" #118

* "Proclaim a Fast!" #689

* "Proclaim Liberty!" #696

* "Prodigal Son!, The" #641

* "Progress! (K.A.N. Ch. 18)" #516

* "Promised Land!, The (Acts 13:4)" #46

* "Proof at Last! (MO-ED)" #735

* "Prophecies of the Great Queen" #331A

* "Prophecies of the Handmaiden of the Lord" #19

* "Sacrificial Lambton—On the Alter of Watergate" #239

* "Saddest Christmas Day?, The" #654

* "Sahara!" #388

* "Sample, Not a Sermon, A" #J

* "Saul and Michael" #115

* "Say 'Goodbye' to Children!" #608

* "Scatteration!" #318

* "Schedules" #106

* "School, The" #165

* "Scriptures on Marriage, Divorce and Remarriage" #Q

* "Secret!, The" #845

* "Secret Weapon, The" #358

* "Security in God's Kingdom, and the Pier" #364

* "Security Rules! (FN 9:11)" #761

* "Seduced! (K.A.N. Ch. 14)" #512

* "Seek First!" #697

* "Sequel to 'Musical Key'" #326A

* "7 Supporters!" #673

* "7 Ways to Know God's Will!" #829

* "7000 Years of World History!—Part I" #645

* "7000 Years of World History!—Part II" #693

* "7000 Years of World History!—Part III" #694

* "'78 Here We Come!" #658

* "70 Years Prophecy of the End, The" #156

* "Sex in Heaven!" #818

* "Sex Problems!" #332C

* "Sex Questions 1" #815

* "Sex Questions 2" #816

* "Sex Questions 3" #816-2

* "Sex Works!" #306

* "Sergeant York!" #849

* "Shah's Last Resort, The" #733

* "Shake-Up, The" #328C

* "Shangri-La—Lost Horizon Found" #228

* "Share the Know" #301A

* "Shepherdess!, The" #837

* "Shepherd's Crook, The" #99

* "Shepherd's Rod!, The" #682

* "Shepherd-Time Story, A" #113

* "Shiners?—Or Shamers?" #241

* "Shtick" #703

* "Sinking Boat Dream, The" #354

* "Sinking Truck!, The: The Church Ministry" #848-1

* "Sinking Truck!, The: The Dangers of Going to Church!" #848-2

* "Sinking Truck!, The: The Mobile Ministry!" #848-3

* "Skylab and the Oil War!" #801

* "Snake Charmer!, The" #557

* "Snowman" #195

* "Snowman Colouring Book" #336

* "Sock It to Me!—That's the Spirit!" #32

* "Solaris" #271

* "Son of Sam" #764

* "Sorry Judas! It's Too Late to Quit! (NRS 16)" #772

* "Sounds in the Night" #85

* "So You Want to be a Leader?" #31

* "Space City" #75A

* "Spaceship!" #624

* "Special 'Emergency Notice to All Leaders of All Colonies!'" #168A

* "Special Police Powers" #219

* "Specifice" #127

* "Spider's Web, The" #227

* "Spirit of God, The" #337

* "Spirit Tree" #194

* "Spiritual Communications" #341

* "Spirit World!, The" #622

* "Sprint Centre Monthly Report Form" #668

* "Squeeze!--Don't Jerk!" #11

* "Stand in the Gap (Ezekiel 22:30)" #70

* "State of the Nation" #197

* "State of the World" #270

* "Statistics" #141

* "Stop—Look--Listen!" #74

* "Strange Bedfellows!" #634

* "Strange Truths" #360

* "Students Stand Up!" #299

* "Suggestions" #124

* "Survival" #172

* "Survival for Families!" #859

* "Sword of the Lord, The" #309A

* "Taming the Baby! (K.A.N. Ch. 16)" #514

* "Tangled Lines of Hejaz!, The" #625

* "Tape—Analysis of 'Time' Article" #153A

* "Tape 1 (God's Little Miracles Part I)" #1

* "Tape 2 (God's Little Miracles Part II)" #2

* "Tape 3 (Follow God!)" #4

* "Tape 4" #17

* "Tape 5 (Afif)" #43

* "Taurgu!" #616

* "Teamwork!" #553

* "Techi's Story—Chapter 1" #785

* "Techi's Story—Chapter 2" #786

* "Techi's Story—Chapter 3: 'Home or Hospital?'" #787

* "Techi's Story—Chapter 4" #788

* "Techi's Story—Chapter 5: 'Birth Miracles!'" #789

* "Techi's Story—Chapter 6: 'Dito Meets Techi!'" #790

* "Techi's Story—Chapter 7: 'Where Do Babies Come From?'" #794

* "Techi's Story—Chapter 8: 'Heavenly Techi'" #795

* "Techi's Story—Chapter 9: 'Recovery!'" #827

* "Techi's Story—Chapter 10: 'Breastfeeding!'" #863

* "Techi's Story—Chapter 11: 'Convalescence!'" #864

* "Techi's Welcome to Spain (FN 10:5)" #760

* "Telephone Traitors and Problem Pastors (MWWFL Nos. 19 and 20)" #315A

* "Temple Prophecy, The" #9

* "Temple Time" #191

* "Tents and Sleeping Bags, Part 1 and 2" #861

* "Terror by Night!" #857

* "Thanks and Comments" #157

* "There Are Absolutes!" #376

* "There Are No Neutrals" #F

* "They Behold His Face!" #397

* "They Can't Stop Our Rain!" #128

* "35MM Negs!" #356

* "Thoughts and Prophecies" #116

* "Timothy Revelation, The" #784

* "Timothy's Departure" #778

* "Tithe, The" #702

* "To All My Children—With Love!" #100

* "To Europe with Love" #101

* "To My Sons of All Colours" #105

* "To My Typewriter Queens" #301B

* "To Our Worldwide Family" #307A

* "To Pacific's Former Leaders (FN 2:2)" #821

* "To the Media, From a Guru!" #800

* "To the Northwest Brethren" #109

* "To Whom Shall We Go?" #862

* "Training and Shepherding Babes (MO-ED)" #734

* "Trans-Iberian Canal, The" #393

* "Treasure Ship!" #614

* "Tree, The" #319

* "TRF-IRF Stat and LLIMM Revolution!, The" #810

* "Trouble with the System is: Problems!" #840

* "Truth!—Vs. 112 Official Lies, The" #317

* "Tunnel and the Call to Arms! (K.A.N.Ch17)" #510

* "Ultimate Trip, The" #80

* "Uncircumcision" #782

* "Uneager Beaver, The" #352

* "Unguarded Moment, The" #838

* "Use It! (Dropouts III)" #27

* "U.S. Merchant Submarine, The" #355

* "U.S. Stooges" #741

* "Vanity Fair" #170

* "Victory! (K.A.N. Ch. 17)" #515

* "War and Peace—Or, What Has Communism Got?" #255

* "War—Boom—Bust!" #H

* "War Has Begun!, The" #869

* "Warning!" #655

* "Warning Notice! (Re: LIMS)" #871

* "Warning on Distribution of Controversial Literature" #274A

* "Warning to All Mail Box Litnessers!" #895

* "Watch, The" #186A

* "'What Every Driver Should Know!'—Chapter One: Brakes and Bearings" #851-1

* "'What Every Driver Should Know!'—Chapter Six: Battery Care and Starting!" #851-6

* "'What Every Driver Should Know!'—Chapter Two: Oil, Water and Tire Pressure" #851-2

* "'What Every Driver Should Know!'—Chapter Three: The Daily Check!" #851-3

* "'What Every Driver Should Know!'—Chapter Five: The Overhaul" #851-5

* "'What Every Driver Should Know!'—Chapter Four: Time for a Tune-up!" #851-4

* "What Is That in Thy Hand!" #315

* "What Now?!—Persecution and Fleeing (NRS 2)" #748

* "What's the Difference?" #330C

* "What To!" #332A

* "When I'm Gone" #706

* "When Is 'Sin' Not Sin?" #594

* "When Morning Dawns!" #852

* "When To!" #332B

* "Where Are the Shepherds?" #662

* "You Are What You Read—Part I" #775

* "Your Declaration of Independence" #173

* "Your 2-Year Old Can Receive Jesus" #708

C. LETTERS NOT YET GENERALLY AVAILABLE

These are Mo-Letters which have been published in or advertised in COG periodicals, but as yet are not part of any volume of letters. Several are numbered in the 900s while others are still unnumbered.

962. Berg, David. "Dear Friend or Foe." FAMILY NEWS. Zurich: World Services, February 1980. p. 1.

963. ———. "The Easter Story!" FAMILY NEWS, 37 (1 April 1981) 7-30, 37-44.

964. ———. "The Trouble with the Tropics!" n.p., n.d.

965. ———. "Video Vision!" FAMILY NEWS, 37 (1 April 1981) 45.

Mo-letter #971-DFO.

966. ———. "Videos!" FAMILY NEWS, 37 (1 April 1981) 49-56.

Mo-letter #964-DO.

967. Berg, David and Maria. "Latest News Flashes!" FAMILY NEWS, 37 (1 April 1981) 2-5.

Mo-letter #973-DO.

D. RETITLED LETTERS

These are Mo-Letters which have been revised from the originals and republished under new titles. In some cases only the pictures are changed, while for other letters the texts have been rewritten.

968. Berg, David. "Are You?" POORKID MAGAZINE, 2 (1974) 12.

Corresponds to item 199.

969. ------. "Beauty for Ashes." n.p.: The Children of God, 1973. 2 pp.

Corresponds to item 265.

970. ------. "The Candle." n.p.: The Children of God, 14 February 1971. 2 pp.

Corresponds to item 15.

971. ------. "The Family of Love." NEW NATION NEWS, 1 (July 1977) 21-25.

Corresponds to item 508.

972. ------. "Good Sport!" POORKID MAGAZINE, 4 (1975) 6-9.

Corresponds to item 207.

973. ------. "Insane Dreamers." n.p., 24 April 1971.

Corresponds to item 88.

974. ------. "Its So Simple!" POORKID MAGAZINE, 7 January 1979) 9-10.

Corresponds to item 534.

975. ------. "Love for All!: True Komix." LOVE IS NEWS!, 1 (April 1981) 5-7.

Corresponds to item 508.

976. ------. "Mighty Mo and the Spirit World!: Flatlanders." POORKID MAGAZINE, 4 (1975) 12-18.

Corresponds to item 78.

977. ------. "Mighty Mo and the Spirit World!: Musical Key." POORKID MAGAZINE, 5 (1976) 6-12.

Corresponds to item 399.

978.   ——. "The Missile War!" London: The Children of God, 1973. 1 p.

        Corresponds to item 312.

979.   ——. "The Only Gift for Christmas!" NEW NATION NEWS, 11
        (December 1977) p. 7 of the supplement.

        Corresponds to item 223.

980.   ——. "Survival or the True Story of Moses and the Children of God.
        First Authentic History of the Jesus Revolution." Bromley, Kent,
        England: Children of God Publications, 1972. 40 pp.

        Corresponds to item 199.

981.   ——. "The Warning Prophesy." n.p., n.d.

        Corresponds to item 672.

982.   ——. "Wild and Free!" POORKID MAGAZINE, 4 (1975) 10-11.

        Corresponds to item 223.

983.   ——. "You Never Lose by Giving!" NEW NATIONS NEWS, 1 (November
        1977) 22-29.

        Corresponds to item 547.

E. COLLECTED LETTERS

The Mo-Letters have also been published in collected form. A series of nine volumes contain over 1000 letters, and are published in leather bound, Bible like form. Other sets of letters have been published in booklet form. Those collected letters appearing in magazines have been referenced as journal articles. Those published independently have been referenced as books.

984. Berg, David. ABRAHIM THE GYPSY KING! Rome: The Children of God, 1977. 11 pp.

Contains items 331, 333, and 336.

985. ------. THE AMERICAN NIGHTMARE. Bromley, Kent, England: The Children of God Trust, 1973. 7 pp.

Contains items 249, 250, 251, and 252.

986. ------. THE BASIC MO LETTERS. Hong Kong: Gold Lion, October 1976. 1521 pp.

Contains 144 letters.

987. ------. THE BOOK OF REVELATION! Sydney: The Children of God, 1976. 63 pp.

Contains items 504, 541, and 548.

988. ------. CHANGE THE WORLD! 2. Hong Kong: Gold Lion, 1977. 94 pp.

Contains items 565, 2, 433, and 584.

989. ------. GADDAFI! EARTH'S LAST PHAROAH? Seattle: Children of God Publications, 1973. 16 pp.

Contains items 129, 275, 273, 276, and an unnumbered work with the same title as the phamphlet.

990. ------. "Give a Little ... and You'll ... Get a Lot!" POORKID MAGAZINE, 4 (1975) 3-5.

Contains items 353 and 301.

991. ------. GIVE A LITTLE GET A LOT. Hong Kong: Wild Wind Productions, 1977. 92 pp. Wild Wind Book No. GP-1005.

Contains items 369, 439, 408, 412, 449, 370 and 572.

992.   ——. THE GREEN DOOR AND THE 'DRUG STORE' — TWO SPIRIT
        TRIPS. London: Children of God, 1973. 13 pp.

        Contains items 292 and 296.

993.   ——. "It's All in the Eyeball!" POORKID MAGAZINE, 2 (1974) 10-11.

        Contains items 346 and 349.

994.   ——. ISLAM! n.p., n.d.

        Contains items 648 and 726.

995.   ——. IT'S LIKE BEING A LITTLE BIT PREGNANT. Hong Kong: Wild
        Wind Productions, 1977. 92 pp. Wild Wind Book No. GP-1001.

        Contains Items 13, 111, 340 and 366.

996.   ——. KING OF THE BEGGARS. Hong Kong: Wild Wind Productions,
        1977. 92 pp.

        Contains items 108, 101, 102, 103, 171, 175 and 534.

997.   ——. LETTERS FROM MOSES DAVID TO THE CHILDREN OF GOD.
        London: Children of God Publications, 1974. 96 pp.

        Contains items 47, 27, 15, 22, 25, 78, 30, 97, 268, 95, 13, 198, 52, 138,
        183, 227, 44, 37, 98, 170, and 199.

998.   ——. LOOK OF LOVE. Hong Kong: Gold Lion, 1977. 94 pp.

        Contains items 349, 346, 894, 509 and 533.

999.   ——. LOVE AT FIRST SIGHT. Hong Kong: Wild Wind Productions,
        1977. 92 pp. Wild Wind Book No. GP-1002.

        Contains items 346, 348 and 349.

1000.   ——. LOVE FOR ALL, ALL FOR LOVE! Zurich: World Services, 1978.
        4 pp.

        Contains items 508 and 591.

1001.   ——. LOVE LETTERS! Rome: The Family of Love, 1978. 32 pp.

        Contains a collection of letters.

1002.   ——. "Menachem Begin—Israel's End? NEW NATION NEWS, 10 (1977)
        16-17.

        Contains a collection of letters.

1003.   ——. THE MO LETTERS A-150, VOL. I. Hong Kong: Gold Lion
        Publishers, 1977. 1228 pp.

1004.   ———. THE MO LETTERS 151-300, VOL. II. Hong Kong: Gold Lion
Publishers, 1977. 2433 pp.

1005.   ———. THE MO LETTERS 301-400, VOL. III. Hong Kong: Gold Lion
Publishers, July 1976. 3680 pp.

1006.   ———. THE MO LETTERS 601-700, VOL. V. Zurich: World Services,
1979.

1007.   ———. THE MO LETTERS 701-800, VOL. VI. Zurich: World Services,
n.d.

1008.   ———. THE MO LETTERS 801-900, VOL. VII. Zurich: World Services,
n.d.

1009.   ———. THE MO LETTERS 901-1000, VOL VIII. n.p, 1981.

1010.   ———. THE PICTORAL BASIC MO-LETTER CATALOGUE: OF THE
BASIC 150 MO-LETTERS! n.p., n.d.

1011.   ———. REAL LOVE! Rome: The Family of Love, 1978. 18 pp.

Contains a collection of letters.

1012.   ———. THE REBELLION OF DAVID: QUOTATIONS FROM MO.
Seattle: Children of God Trust, 1973. 16 pp.

Contains items 255, 61, 2, 15, 9, 5, 143, 272, 275, 25, 88, 90, 31, 96,
54, 203, 103, and 285, excerpts only.

1013.   ———. SHARING REAL LOVE! Rome: The Family of Love, 1978. 18
pp.

Contains a collection of letters.

1014.   ———. THOUGHTS FROM CHAIRMAN MO. Hong Kong: Gold Lion,
1976. 220 pp.

Contains excerpts from the 144 letters of item 986.

1015.   ———. THOUGHTS FROM MO QUOTE BOOK. Hong Kong: Gold Lion,
n.d.

Contains excerpts from the 144 letters of item 986.

1016.   ———. 3 MO LETTERS ON THE GREAT COMET: WARNING! London:
The Children of God, 1973. 6 pp.

Contains items 299, 311 and 313.

1017.   ———. TO HELL WITH THE PROPER WAY. Hong Kong: Wild Wind
Productions, 1977. 92 pp.

Contains items 31, 54, 61 and 129.

1018.   ———. THE VISIONS OF DANIEL. Sydney: The Children of God, n.d.
47 pp.

Contains items 448, 451, 452, 453 and 454.

1019.   ------. THE WORLD TODAY AND TOMORROW! 'THOUGHTS FROM
        CHAIRMAN MO.' n.p., n.d.

        Contains items 420 and 424.

1020.   David, Deborah, Mother Eve David, Faith David and the Mo Education
        Classes.   CHILDREN OF GOD PUBLICATIONS CATALOGUE. n.p.,
        1976.

        Contains excerpts from a number of letters.

II

COG PUBLICATIONS

The COG has been one of the most prodigious producers of literature among the Jesus People groups. Throughout its history, the production and distribution of literature has been one of its major methods of outreach, and often has appeared to be the exclusive focus of the group's energies.

A. LETTERS NOT BY DAVID BERG

A number of letters have been written by COG leaders other than Berg. Like the Mo-Letters, these have been classified according to intended audience and numbered in series. Because all of these letters are not cited, the items are listed alphabetically only. The authors are as follows: Eve Berg (Mother Eve David) is David Berg's first wife; Deborah David and Faith David are his daughters, Sara Davidito is one of his concubines, and John Trendwell (Jethro Levi) is his son-in-law.

1021. Apollos and David Berg (Moses David). "The Big Lie!" Chicago: The Children Of God, 1977. 18 pp. #3-GP.

1022. Berg, Eve (Mother Eve David). "Condemnation." n.p., n.d. #10.

1023. ———. "Creation Revelation." n.p., n.d. #16.

1024. ———. "Dreams." n.p., n.d. #38.

1025. ———. "Freedom in the Spirit." n.p., n.d. #7.

1026. ———. "Getting Things From God." n.p., n.d. #39.

1027. ———. "The Honesty Revolution." London: The Children of God, 1973. 2 pp. #34-LTO.

1028. ———. "In the Beginning ... Sex!" NEW NATION NEWS, 7 (Spring 1974) 6. #22

1029. ———. "Leading Our Children." n.p., n.d. #30.

1030. ———. "Praise." n.p., n.d. #1.

1031. ———. "The Sex Revolution." London: The Children of God, 1973. 1 p. #34A-LTO.

1032. Berg, Virginia Brandt (Grandmother). "BACA." n.p.: The Children of God, September 1976. 2 pp. #MM1:1-GP.

1033. ——. "Boomerang." n.p.: The Children of God, April 1977. 2 pp. #MM1:2-GP.

1034. ——. "Precious Promises." n.p.: The Children of God, April 1977. 2 pp. #MM1:3-GP.

1035. ——. "It's So Because God Said So!" Rome: The Family of Love, July 1978. 6 pp. #MM2:2 and 4:6-DFO.

1036. Carlos. "Confessions of an Intellectual." n.p.: The Children of God, 1976. 12 pp. #FD60.

Contains Carlos' story (his last name is not given) with an introduction by Faith David.

1037. David, Deborah. "Faith for a Little Child." n.p., n.d. #DD15.

1038. ——. "The Joy of Childbirth—Natural Childbirth Part II: 'Understanding the Process of Labour.'" Sydney: The Children of God, 1975. 36 pp. #DD18.

1039. ——. "The Miracle of Life—Natural Childbirth Part I: Education." Sydney: The Children of God, 1975. 37 pp. #DD17.

1040. ——. "An Ounce of Prevention Is Worth a Pound of Cure." n.p., n.d. #DD9.

1041. ——. "Teach Me Lord to Pray!" n.p., n.d. #DD16.

1042. David, Faith. "Letter to the Underground Church in America." n.p., n.d. #29.

1043. ——. "9 Hours with Gaddafi!" n.p., n.d. #22.

1044. ——. "A Shepherd's Confession." n.p., n.d. #10.

1045. ——. "Witnessing Tips." n.p., n.d. #7.

1046. Davidito, Sara. "Feed My Lambs!—Part 1." Rome: The Family of Love, 1978. 5 pp. #S16-DFO.

1047. Trendwell, John (Jethro Levi). "Responsible Leadership." London: The Children of God, 1974. #JL2-DFO.

1048. Wind, Shua Wild. "An Oriental Jesus." Sydney: Pacific Publications, 1975. #4-DO.

1049. ——. "Counseling." Sydney: Pacific Publications, n.d. #5-DO.

1050. ——. "Pioneer Schools." Sydney: Pacific Publications, n.d.

1051. ——. "Pump Initiative Power!" Sydney: Pacific Publications, n.d.

1052. ——. "Small Colony Clubs." Sydney: Pacific Publications, 1975. #3-DFO.

1053. ——. "What's Your Standard?" Sydney: Pacific Publications, n.d. #2-DFO.

B. MAGAZINE ARTICLES

These are representative articles from some of the COG periodicals. Subjects covered range from testimonies, instructional material, and practical tips to group doctrine.

1054. Berg, David (Moses David). "Give It Away!" NEW NATION NEWS, 8 (1976) 13-14.

1055. ------. "How to Cure Headaches." POORKID MAGAZINE, 3, n.d.

1056. ------. "Mo's 'Love Chapter'!" NEW NATION NEWS, 7 (Spring 1974) 10.

1057. Cartoon, Jacob. "No Longer Kung-Fu-sed!" POORKID MAGAZINE, 4 (1975) 9.

1058. The Children of God. "Favorite Christmas Carols." NEW NATION NEWS, 11 (December 1977) supplement, 6 pp.

1059. Inkletter, Hart. "Handlettering." FAMILY NEWS, 37 (1 April 1981) 65-66.

C. BOOKS

The subject matter of COG books ranges from selected sections of Mo-Letters, instructional material, and stories of interest to evangelistic messages. In addition to David Berg, the authors are as follows: Virginia Brandt Berg is his mother; Cephas and Samson Warner are COG leaders, and Miguel is a COG convert.

1060. Berg, David (Moses David). CONDENSED QUOTES FROM THE LOVE LETTERS OF FATHER DAVID. n.p., n.d.

A Mini Books series.

1061. ———. DAILY MIGHT NO. 1. Hong Kong: The Children of God, 1976 and The Family of Love, 1978. 31 pp.

1062. ———. DAILY MIGHT NO. 2. Hong Kong: The Family of Love, 1977 and 1978. 31 pp.

1063. ———. DAILY MIGHT NO. 3. Hong Kong: The Family of Love, 1978. 31 pp.

1064. ———. DFO KOMIX BOOK. Zurich: World Services, 1981.

1065. ———. THE FF-ER'S HANDBOOK. n.p., January 1977.

1066. ———. HEALING BOOK. n.p, n.d. 128 pp.

1067. ———. IT'S A BOY (THE STORY OF LITTLE DAVID). n.p. n.d.

1068. ———. KOMIX ONE. Zurich: World Services, 1981.

Contains True Komix #1-68.

1069. ———. KOMIX TWO. Zurich: World Services, 1981. Nearly 800 pp.

Contains True Komix #69-180.

1070. ———. KOMIX THREE. Zurich: World Services, 1981.

1071. ———. NEW LIFE—NEW LOVE! Rome: The Family of Love, June 1978. 21 pp.

1072. Berg, David (Moses David) and Joel Wordsworth. THE REVOLUTION FOR JESUS. n.p.: The Children of God Publications, 1972. Over 51 pp.

1073. Berg, Virginia Brandt. THE PROMISES OF GOD ARE STREAMS THAT
       NEVER RUN DRY. Amsterdam: Children of God Publications, 1972.
       48 pp.

1074. Cephas. KIDNAPPED. n.p., n.d.

1075. The Children of God. ATTACK WITH THE WORD! WILD WIND WORD
       TAPES CATALOGUE 81. Zurich: World Services, 1981. 7 pp.

1076. ———. BASIC COURSE. Zurich: World Services, 1981.

1077. ———. BIBLE KNOWLEDGE. Sydney: Pacific Publications, n.d.

1078. ———. BOOK OF TECHI STORIES. Zurich: World Services, 1981.

1079. ———. DITO SERIES. Zurich: World Services, 1981.

1080. ———. THE EMERGENCY SURVIVAL MANUAL. Dallas: Children of
       God, 1974. 76 pp.

1081. ———. FAMILY CARE BOOK. n.p., n.d.

1082. ———. FAMILY DEVOTIONAL POETRY. Zurich: World Services, 1981.

1083. ———. FAMILY NEWS. Zurich: World Services, 1981. 188 pp.

1084. ———. FAMILY NEWS—SPECIAL INTRODUCTORY ISSUE. Zurich:
       World Services, February 1980, 15 pp.

1085. ———. FAMILY REFERENCE BOOK. Zurich: World Services, 1981.

1086. ———. FIRST PRINCIPLES OF THE REVOLUTION FOR JESUS!
       Amsterdam: Children of God Publications, 1972. 104 pp.

1087. ———. FLANNELGRAPH MAG 2. Zurich: World Services, 1981. Over
       200 pp.

1088. ———. MINI BOOKS. n.p., n.d.

1089. ———. OUR NEW FAMILY SONGBOOK. Zurich: World Services, 1981.

1090. ———. PREGNANCY THRU SCHOOL DAYS. VOL. 1. Zurich: World
       Services, 1981.

1091. ———. QUOTEBOOK. Zurich: World Services, 1981.

1092. ———. REVOLUTION FOR JESUS—HOW TO DO IT. n.p.: Essen, 1973.

1093. ———. THE SHEPHERD'S MANUAL. Sydney: Pacific Publications, n.d.

1094. ———. STUDY AND REFERENCE HELPS BOOK. n.p., n.d.

1095. Miguel. MIGUEL'S TESTIMONY. Melbourne: The Children of God,
       1977. 30 pp.

1096. Theophilus, Paul (compiler). A'RITHMETIC REVOLUTION. Rome: Flee School Creations, 1976. 11 pp.

1097. ------. TEACHING GENERAL SCIENCE. Rome: Flee School Creations, 1976. 19 pp.

1098. ------. TEACHING TIPS. Rome: The Children of God, 1976. 19 pp.

1099. Warner, Samson. WE ARE THE CHILDREN OF GOD! Melbourne: World Services, 1977. 32 pp.

D. BOOKLETS

Booklets have been published on a variety of topics. The items called "sets" are collected Scripture references, some items are evangelistic messages, and others are topical classes for members.

1100. Berg, David. DAVID SERIES. n.p., n.d. 16 pp. #BL1

1101. ------. GREEN DOOR. n.p., n.d. 12 pp. #BL4.

1102. ------. GREEN PAPER PIG. n.p., n.d. 16 pp. #BL3.

1103. ------. LETTERS FROM A SHEPHERD. n.p., n.d. #LFS1

1104. ------. MO VIEWS THE NEWS. n.p., n.d. 16 pp. #BL2.

1105. Berg, Virginia B. THE HEM OF HIS GARMENT. n.p., n.d. #VB2.

1106. ------. STREAMS THAT NEVER RUN DRY. n.p., n.d. #VB1.

1107. The Children of God. A NEW WORLD FOR LITTLE PEOPLE. Rome: Children of God Childcare Publications, n.d. 21 pp.

1108. ------. BASIC CLASS BOOK VOL. 1. n.p., n.d. #CB1.

1109. ------. CHALLENGE OF THE CHILDREN. n.p., n.d. #PR2.

1110. ------. THE CHILDREN ON THE MOVE. n.p., n.d. #PR3.

1111. ------. GOD BLESS YOU. n.p., n.d.

1112. ------. GOD'S PACKAGE DEAL. n.p., n.d.

1113. ------. IS IT SCRIPTURAL TO WORK FOR MONEY AND WORLDLY RICHE$? n.p., n.d.

1114. ------. SET CARD. Brisbane, Australia: The Children of God. n.d.

1115. ------. SETS 1-10. Zurich: World Services, 1981. #BSC1.

1116. ------. PSALMS AND CHAPTERS. Zurich: World Services, 1981. #BSC2.

1117. ------. ULTIMATE TRIP. n.p., n.d. #PR1.

1118. ------. WITNESSING SETS OF VERSES—FOR MEMORIZATION. Zurich: World Services, 1979. 16 pp.

1119.   Shem. ROLLING THE GOLD: A CLASS ON BUDGETS. Sydney: Pacific
        Publications, 1975.

E. POSTERS AND TRACTS

The PS numbered items are posters of the cover cartoons from their respective Mo-Letters. The TR numbered items, as well as the unnumbered items, are tracts which indirectly derive from Mo-Letters.

1120. Berg, David (Moses David). "Our Symbol! And What It Means!" Rome: The Children of God, 1976. 1 p.

1121. ——. "Give It Away!" n.p., The Children of God, 1974. 2 pp.

1122. Berg, David and Eve Berg (Moses David and Mother Eve). "Christmas — What Does It Mean?" n.p.: The Children of God, 1975. 4 pp.

1123. The Children of God. "A Map Showing Regions of the World for Which COG Bishops Are Responsible." n.p., n.p.

1124. ——. "Are We Living in 'the Time of the End?'" n.p., n.d.

1125. ——. "Baby Tract—English." n.p., n.d. #TR2.

1126. ——. "Bye, Bye, Miss American Pie." n.p., n.d. #PS2.

1127. ——. "Don Quixote." n.p., n.d. #PS4.

1128. ——. "Endtime Tract." n.p., n.d. #TR4.

1129. ——. "Flashback Funnies Tract." n.p., n.d. #TR7.

1130. ——. "Gaddafi's Third World." n.p., n.d. #PS1.

1131. ——. "God Bless You." n.p., n.d.

1132. ——. "Green Paper Pig." n.p., n.d. #PS5.

1133. ——. "Imitation Salvation Tract." n.p., n.d. #TR6.

1134. ——. "International Baby Tract." n.p., n.d. #TR1.

1135. ——. "The Life Story of Virginia Brandt Berg." n.p., n.d.

1136. ——. "Monthly FF Witnessing Report." n.p., n.d.

1137. ——. "Mountin' Maid." n.p., n.d. #PS6.

1138. ——. "A Prophecy of God on the Old Church and the New Church." London or Dallas: The Children of God, 1973. 4 pp.

1139. ———. "Revolutionary Contract (Revolutionary Sheet)." n.p., n.d.

1140. ———. "Revolutionary Sex." n.p., n.d. #PS7.

1141. ———. "Revolutionary Women." n.p., n.d. #PS3.

1142. ———. "Sweet Pea Tract." n.p., n.d. #TR5.

1143. ———. "This Is the Application Form of the 'Children of God.'" Mingus, Texas: The Children of God, n.d.

1144. ———. "Warning (Warning Tract)." Dallas: The Children of God, n.d. #TR3.

F. PERIODICALS

Over the years the COG has published a number of periodicals with varying formats. While some were fairly plain, others were more polished (i.e., with color pictures, art work etc.). Those publications geared towards friends and supporters have sought to keep them abreast of developments in the group's practices and teachings, and often have made appeals for financial support. Those publications geared towards the general public have usually sought to stimulate interest in the group, offering further information via the mail.

Most of the periodicals have been discontinued or replaced over time due to financial problems and/or changes of emphasis in the group's approach to outreach. Others have been phased out inorder to be replaced by a periodical with a different format.

Information on the dates of publication and whether periodicals are still available has been given whenever it was known.

1145. FAMILY NEWS. Zurich: World Services.

Published monthly. The first issue was pre-1976. The last issue was the issue prior to Vol. 8, No. 2 of New Nation News, into which it was incorporated. It includes: news, practical tips, testimony, children's exercises, Mo letters, poems, articles, want ads, warnings about excommunicated members, etc.

1146. KIDZ MAGAZINE. Zurich: World Services.

Published monthly. The first issue was 1981.

1147. 'KRAKATON.' News of the South Pacific. Sydney: The Children of God.

It includes: pictures, information, tips on litnessing, etc.

1148. LEADER'S MAGAZINE. n.p., n.d.

1149. LOVE IN ACTION! Rome: The Family of Love.

The first issue was June, 1978. It includes: worldwide news for friends, followers and members, letters, etc.

1150. LOVE IS NEWS. Rome: World Services.

Published quarterly at first, later monthly. The first issue was April 1978. It includes: news, testimonies and pictures, etc.

1151. MEXICO REGION NEWSLETTER. n.p., n.d.

1152. NEW IMPROVED TRUTH. n.p., n.d.

1153. NEW NATION NEWS! Chicago: The Children of God, and Rome: World Services.

Published monthly (International Editions in 10 languages). The first issue was either pre-Spring 1974 or else July 1977. It includes: music news, worldwide news, pictures and information on new members, births, childcare tips, marriages, testimonials, letters, etc.

1154. POORKID MAGAZINE. Sydney: Wild Wind Productions; and Melbourne, Christchurch, and Rome: The Children of God.

1155. TRUE COMIX. Rome: The Children of God.

1156. TRUE KOMIX. Zurich: The Children of God.

G. CHILDREN'S LITERATURE

1. MO-LETTERS—CHILDREN'S EDITIONS

The Children's editions of the Mo-Letters have large bold type face and illustrations on each page. They contain selected Mo-Letters which have been revised for this format.

1157. Berg, David (Moses David). "Abrahim." n.p., n.d.

Corresponds to items 331, 333 and 336.

1158. ——. "Alice." n.p., n.d.

Corresponds to item 325.

1159. ——. "Be So Happy." n.p., n.d.

Corresponds to item 183.

1160. ——. "Bewitched." n.p., n.d.

Corresponds to item 326.

1161. ——. "The Bible in Pictures, Vol. I: The Creation and Fall of Man! And Noah and the Flood!" Chicago: Children of God, 1977. 9 pp.

1162. ——. "The Bible in Pictures, Vol. II: The Tower of Babel! And the Life of Abraham!" Chicago: Children of God, 1977. 15 pp.

1163. "The Bible in Pictures, Vol. III: Lot and His Wife! And Isaac and Ismael!" Chicago: Children of God, 1977. 15 pp.

1164. ——. "But if Not." n.p., n.d.

Corresponds to item 366.

1165. ——. "The City of Buried Treasure." n.p., n.d.

Corresponds to item 394.

1166. ——. "Communion." n.p., n.d.

Corresponds to item 441.

1167. ——. "Did God Make a Mistake." n.p., n.d.

Corresponds to item 54.

1168.   ——. "Dumps." n.p., n.d.

 Corresponds to item 52.

1169.   ——. "Faith." n.p., n.d.

 Corresponds to item 95.

1170.   ——. "Glamour or Glory!" n.p., n.d.

 Corresponds to item 404.

1171.   ——. "The Great Escape." n.p., n.d.

 Corresponds to item 184.

1172.   ——. "The Green Paper Pig." n.p., n.d.

 Corresponds to item 273.

1173.   ——. "Hamburger Boat." n.p., n.d.

 Corresponds to item 445.

1174.   ——. "Love Never Fails." n.p., n.d.

 Corresponds to item 44.

1175.   ——. "The Name of Jesus!" n.p., n.d.

 Corresponds to item 450.

1176.   ——. "Rolled Gold." n.p., n.d.

 Corresponds to item 425.

1177.   ——. "The Shepherd's Crook." n.p., n.d.

 Corresponds to item 123.

1178.   ——. "Snowman." n.p., n.d.

 Corresponds to item 224.

1179.   ——. "Stop-Look-Listen." n.p., n.d.

 Corresponds to item 97.

1180.   ——. "Tommy." n.p., n.d.

1181.   ——. "Where Poppies Grow." n.p., n.d.

 Corresponds to item 474.

2. CHILDREN'S READERS

The individual children's readers are called Revolutionary Readers, Mo Science Series, or The Adventures of David Series and are based upon "true-life" incidents taken from the Mo-Letters. They are illustrated and have large typeface for increasing reading ability and "building faith." The Mo Lion Readers are a series of 20 primary readers using the flash card word recognition method for teaching young children to read, two years old and up. They are illustrated and come with flash card word books.

1182. Berg, David (Moses David). ALONE IN LONDON! n.p., n.d.

1183. ------. THE 'BIG DOG' STORY. Rome: Free School Creations, n.d. 11 pp.

1184. ------. DAVID BUILDS A CHURCH. Rome: Free School Creations, 1976. 15 pp.

1185. ------. THE FARMER. Rome: Free School Creations, 1977. 15 pp.

1186. ------. GOD CARES. n.p., n.d.

1187. ------. HURRICANE! Rome: Free School Creations, 1977. 13 pp.

1188. ------. MO LION READER NO. 1: I LIKE TO READ FLASH CARD WORD BOOK. Rome: Free School Creations, 1976. 18 pp.

1189. ------. MO LION READER NO. 2: I LIKE TO READ FLASH CARD WORD BOOK. Rome: Free School Creations, 1976. 30 pp.

1190. ------. SALVATION IS SIMPLE. Rome: Free School Creations, 1976. 15 pp.

1191. ------. TRAPPED ON A MOUNTAIN! n.p., n.d.

3. CHILDREN'S COLORING BOOKS

These coloring books, with the exception of the last item, are based on selected Mo-Letters. The NNN coloring books, item 3057, is based upon the New Nation News periodical.

1192.   Berg, David (Moses David). "Alice and the Magic Garden." n.p.: World Services, n.d.

Corresponds to item 325.

1193.   ------. "Beauty for Ashes." Zurich: World Services, n.d.

Corresponds to item 138.

1194.   ------. "Bye, Bye Birdie." n.p.: World Services, n.d.

Corresponds to item 261.

1195.   ------. "The Crystal Stream." Zurich: World Services, n.d.

Corresponds to item 466.

1196.   ------. "Demonography." Zurich: World Services, n.d.

Corresponds to item 275A.

1197.   ------. "The Green Paper Pig." Zurich: World Services, n.d.

Corresponds to item 273.

1198.   ------. "Holy Holes." n.p.: World Services, n.d.

Corresponds to item 267.

1199.   ------. "Listening? Or Lamenting?" Zurich: World Services, n.d.

Corresponds to item 389.

1200.   ------. "My Love Legend Colour Book." Zurich: World Services, n.d. 16 pp.

Corresponds to item 108.

1201.   ------. "Prayer." n.p.: World Services, n.d.

Corresponds to item 475.

COG Publications

1202. ———. "Richman, Poorman." Zurich: World Services, n.d.

Corresponds to item 390.

1203. ———. "Revolutionary ABC's." n.p.: World Services, n.d.

1204. ———. "The Rose." n.p.: World Services, n.d.

Corresponds to item 265.

1205. ———. "Snowman." n.p.: World Services, n.d.

Corresponds to item 224.

1206. ———. "Sounds in the Night." n.p.: World Services, n.d.

Corresponds to item 109.

1207. ———. "Space City." n.p.: World Services, n.d.

Corresponds to item 99.

1208. ———. "The Spider's Web." Zurich: World Services, n.d.

Corresponds to item 257.

1209. ———. "Squeeze, Don't Jerk." Zurich: World Services, n.d.

Corresponds to item 30.

1210. ———. "Tommy the Little Crippled Boy." n.p.: World Services, n.d.

1211. ———. "Who Is Moses?" Zurich: World Services, n.d.

Corresponds to item 432.

1212. ———. "Colour NNN's." n.p., n.d.

4. CHILDREN'S COMIC BOOKS

Most of the comic books, like the other children's literature, are based on selected Mo-Letters. The True Komix volumes, items 3069 and 3070, are collections of comic books.

1213. Berg, David (Moses David). "The Crash." Zurich: World Services, n.d. 5 pp.

Corresponds to item 319.

1214. ------. "Demonography." Sydney: The Children of God, and Zurich: World Services, 1975. 18 pp.

Corresponds to item 308.

1215. ------. "Diamonds of Dust." n.p., n.d.

Corresponds to item 22.

1216. ------. "The Elixir of Love." n.p., n.d.

Corresponds to item 694.

1217. ------. "Extermination." Rome: The Family of Love, n.d. 7 pp.

Corresponds to item 721.

1218. ------. "The Green Door!" Zurich: World Services, n.d.

Corresponds to item 292.

1219. ------. "Holy Holes." n.p., n.d.

Corresponds to item 267.

1220. ------. "Madame M." n.p.: World Services, n.d.

Corresponds to item 298.

1221. ------. "Mountain Island Villa." Chicago: The Children of God, 1977. 11 pp.

1222. ------. "Poorkid Magazine." n.p.: World Services, n.d.

1223. ------. "The Shepherd's Crook!" n.p., n.d.

Corresponds to item 123.

1224.   ——. "Strange Truths." n.p.: World Services, n.d.

Corresponds to item 465.

1225.   ——. "Students Stand Up!" Chicago: The Children of God, n.d. 4 pp.

Corresponds to item 334.

1226.   ——. "Vanity Fair." n.p.: World Services, n.d.

Corresponds to item 197.

1227.   The Family of Love. "True Komix, Volume I." n.p., n.d.

1228.   ——. "True Komix, Volume II." n.p., n.d.

5. CHILDREN'S BOOKS

These ten books are a series on Scripture memorization for children. Each verse is accompanied by a picture.

1229. The Children of God. CHILDREN'S SCRIPTURE BOOKS: SERIES 1-10. n.p., n.d.

H. AUDIO (CASSETTE TAPES)

The COG has produced some audio materials in series form, dealing with particular themes. Other audio tapes have also been produced singly, without any necessary connection to other works. In the section which follows, because many of the item in the series are not cited, all the tapes have been listed together alphabetically.

Some tapes are credited to David Berg, some to Virginia Brandt Berg (his mother—Grandmother to the Children), and others to the Children of God or the Family of Love. The audio entries have thus been divided into these three author groupings.

Unlike the individual letters, these tapes deal with multiple themes or stories. They have been referenced, therefore, like books.

1230. Berg, David. ABRAHIM THE GYPSY KING; THE GYPSY STORY; GYPSIES ARE ARABS. n.p., 1981. #MLR21.

Contains items 331 and 82.

1231. ——. THE ADVENTURES OF DAVID. FOURTEEN TRUE STORIES FROM THE LIFE OF DAVID. n.p., 1981. #FCT2.

1232. ——. ALICE IN THE MAGIC GARDEN; SPIDER'S WEB. n.p., 1981. #MLR17.

Contains items 325 and 257.

1233. ——. ATTACK; SHEPHERD'S CROOK. n.p., 1981. #MLR33.

Contains items 198 and 123.

1234. ——. Bell, Book and Candle; Choice. n.p., 1981. MLR44.

Contains items 232 and 268.

1235. ——. BIBLE IN PICTURES. n.p., n.d. #MOC5.

Contains items 659, 660, 661 and 749.

1236. ——. THE BIBLE IN PICTURES TAPE 1. CHAPTERS 1 & 2. n.p., 1981. #BP1.

Contains items 659 and 660.

1237. ——. THE BIBLE IN PICTURES TAPE 2. CHAPTERS 3 & 4. n.p., 1981. #BP2.

Contains items 661 and 749.

1238. ———. THE BIBLE IN PICTURES TAPE 3. CHAPTERS 8 & 9. n.p., 1981.
       #BP3.

1239. ———. THE BIBLE IN PICTURES TAPE 4. CHAPTERS 10 & 11. n.p.,
       1981. #BP4.

1240. ———. THE BIBLE IN PICTURES TAPE 5. CHAPTERS 12 & 13. n.p.,
       1981. #BP5.

1241. ———. THE BIBLE IN PICTURES TAPE 6. CHAPTERS 14 & 15. n.p.,
       1981. #BP6.

1242. ———. BIRTHDAY WARNING. n.p., 1981. #MLR5.

1243. ———. THE BOOK OF RUTH. Toulouse Cedex, France: Wild Wind
       Tapes, 1981. #MC15.

1244. ———. BROTHER SUN; RASPUTIN; GOD'S EXPLOSIONS. n.p., 1981.
       #MLR47.

       Contains items 255 and 31.

1245. ———. BUT IF NOT; LETTER TO A LABOURER. n.p., 1981. #MLR37.

       Contains items 366 and 395.

1246. ———. CHANGE THE WORLD, THE ROCK IN THE ROAD; SOUNDS IN
       THE NIGHT WITH SIMON PETER & THE MUSIC WITH MEANING
       FAMILY; THE ANSWER IS LOVE, A PLAY FOR VOICES BY HABAKUK
       2:4 WITH HABAKUK, JOELLA AND MIDIAN. Toulouse Cedex, France:
       Wild Wind Tapes, 1981. #MS2.

       Contains items 572 and 109.

1247. ———. COLONISATION, NOT SCATTERATION. Toulouse Cedex,
       France: Wild Wind Tapes, 1981. #MC10.

       Contains item 3.

1248. ———. COMMUNION WITH DAD. Toulouse Cedex, France: Wild Wind
       Tapes, 1981. #MC21.

1249. ———. CRYSTAL PYRAMID; TEMPLE TIME. n.p., 1981. #MLR20.

       Contains items 243 and 220.

1250. ———. THE DEPRESSION AND SHEPHERDS WITH THE HOT RODS.
       n.p., 1981. #MCC6.

1251. ———. DID GOD MAKE A MISTAKE?; DROPOUTS 1; DROPOUTS 4.
       n.p., 1981. #MLR14.

       Contains item 54.

1252. ——. DUMPS; BE SO HAPPY. n.p., 1981. #MLR11.

Contains items 52 and 183.

1253. ——. THE ELOPEMENT. n.p., 1981. #MCC11.

1254. ——. THE ENDTIME WHISPERING VISION. Toulouse Cedex, France: Wild Wind Tapes, 1981. #MC14 or #MLR34.

Contains item 428.

1255. ——. FAITH AND HEALING; FEET OF FAITH. n.p., 1981. #MLR24.

Contains items 13 and 111.

1256. ——. FIRST CHURCH OF LOVE TAPE; MO'S MUSIC TAPE 4. Toulouse Cedex, France: Wild Wind Tapes, 1981. #MC18.

1257. ——. FLATLANDERS. n.p., 1981. #MLR12.

Contains item 78.

1258. ——. FLIRTY LITTLE FISHY; BEAUTY AND THE BEASTS; THE DANCER. n.p., 1981. #MLR26.

Contains items 353 and 393.

1259. ——. FOR GOD'S SAKE FOLLOW GOD. Toulouse Cedex, France: Wild Wind Tapes, 1981. #MC1.

Contains item 23.

1260. ——. FOR SINNERS LIKE ME, MO'S MUSIC TAPE 3. Toulouse Cedex, France: Wild Wind Tapes, 1981. #MC8.

1261. ——. FORSAKING ALL; BENEFITS OF BACKSLIDING; BACKSLIDING. n.p., 1981. #MLR49.

Contains items 370 and 368.

1262. ——. GETTING ORGANIZED. n.p., 1981. #MLR6.

Contains item 332.

1263. ——. GOD'S LITTLE MIRACLES! TAPE 1 FROM EUROPE. Toulouse Cedex, France: Wild Wind Tapes, 1981. #MC9.

Contains item 20.

1264. ——. GOD'S LITTLE MIRACLES! TAPE 2 FROM EUROPE. Toulouse Cedex, France: Wild Wind Tapes, 1981. #MC12.

1265. ——. GOOD EXECUTIVE. n.p., 1981. MLR3.

1266. ——. GRANDMOTHER'S ACCIDENT. n.p., 1981. #MCC12.

1267. ——. GRANDMOTHER'S OPERATION. n.p., 1981. #MCC13.

1268. ——. GRANDPA'S ACCIDENTS FOR BEING A BAD BOY. n.p., 1981. #MCC2.

1269. ——. GRANDPA'S RANCH STORIES. n.p., 1981. #MCC1.

1270. ——. GRANDPA'S SICKNESS & NEW MODELS. n.p., 1981. #MCC9.

Contains item 941.

1271. ——. GREAT GRANDPA & THE TRAINS & GREAT GRANDPA & THE LADIES. n.p., 1981. #MCC10.

1272. ——. GREEN DOOR; DRUGSTORE. n.p., 1981. #MLR18.

Contains items 292 and 296.

1273. ——. HAVE FAITH, WILL TRAVEL. Toulouse Cedex, France: Wild Wind Tapes, 1981. #MC5.

Contains item 169.

1274. ——. THE HURRICANE. n.p., 1981. #MCC5.

1275. ——. I AM A TOILET; GLAMOUR OR GLORY. n.p., 1981. #MLR38. Contains items 294 and 404.

1276. ——. INTRO TO THE REVOLUTION & OUR BASIC BELIEFS. n.p., 1981. #QB1.

1277. ——. JESUS PEOPLE OR REVOLUTION; EZEKIEL 34. Toulouse Cedex, France: Wild Wind Tapes, 1981. #MC2.

Contains item 167.

1278. ——. KINGS & CASTLES. TWO WONDERFUL WORD STORIES AND TWENTY SCRIPTURE SONGS. n.p., 1981. #FCT1.

1279. ——. LIFE IN THE COLD, THE JOURNEY SOUTH & HEALING THE BABY. n.p., 1981. #MCC4.

1280. ——. LISTENING OR LAMENTING?; BUILDERS BEWARE. n.p., 1981. #MLR28.

Contains items 389 and 355.

1281. ——. LISTENING WITH A PURPOSE. TWELVE LANGUAGE WITH A PURPOSE STORIES. n.p., 1981. #FCT3.

1282. ——. LORD BYRON'S SURRENDER; LOVEMAKING IN THE SPIRIT; WILD WIND; OLD CHURCH, NEW CHURCH. n.p., 1981. #MLR22.

Contains items 339, 16 and 1.

1283. ———. LOVE AND SEX. n.p., 1981. #QB10.

1284. ———. LOVE NEVER FAILS; DIAMONDS OF DUST; ROSE; ALL THINGS CHANGE; SQUEEZE DON'T JERK; BEAUTY FOR ASHES. n.p., 1981. #MLR1.

Contains items 44, 22, 265, 25, 30 and 138.

1285. ———. MADAME M; PSYCHIC SEES THE FUTURE. n.p., 1981. #MLR43.

Contains items 298 and 320.

1286. ———. MO LETTERS! 44 TAPES READ BY SIMON PETER. Toulouse Cedex, France: Wild Wind Tapes, n.d.

1287. ———. MORE ON FAITH. Toulouse Cedex, France: Wild Wind Tapes, 1981. #MC16.

Contains item 960.

1288. ———. MORNING PRAYER; LAW OF LOVE; PRAYER FOR LOVE AND MERCY; MO'S LOVE CHAPTER. n.p., 1981. #MLR4.

Contains items 122, 343 and 98.

1289. ———. MO'S LOVE TAPE, MOUNTAIN' MAID. Toulouse Cedex, France: Wild Wind Tapes, 1981. #MC6.

Contains item 270.

1290. ———. MO'S LOVE TAPE—'MOUNTAIN MAID.' n.p., n.d. #MOC10

Contains item 270.

1291. ———. MO'S MUSIC TAPE 1. Toulouse Cedex, France: Wild Wind Tapes, 1981. #MC3.

1292. ———. MO'S MUSIC TAPE 2. Toulouse Cedex, France: Wild Wind Tapes, 1981. #MC4.

1293. ———. MO'S MUSIC TAPES. n.p., n.d. #MOC6.

1294. ———. MO'S MUSIC TAPES 1, 2 AND #3—'FOR SINNERS LIKE ME.' Toulouse Cedex, France: Wild Wind Tapes, n.d.

1295. ———. MOTION SICKNESS. Toulouse Cedex, France: Wild Wind Tapes, 1981. #MC17.

1296. ———. MOUNTAIN MEN. Toulouse Cedex, France: Wild Wind Tapes, 1981. #MC22.

Contains item 2.

1297. ———. MOUNTAIN MEN; FAITH. n.p., 1981. #MLR25.

Contains items 2 and 95.

1298. ———. MUSICAL KEY; SEQUEL TO MUSICAL KEY. n.p., 1981. #MLR31.

Contains items 399 and 400.

1299. ———. NAME OF JESUS; LET'S TALK ABOUT JESUS; THE TEMPLE PROPHECY. n.p., 1981. #MLR46.

Contains items 450, 39 and 28.

1300. ———. NO MATTER HOW SMALL YOU ARE. EIGHTY-TWO GRANDPA QUOTES PUT TO SONG PLUS OTHERS. n.p., 1981. #FCT5

1301. ———. OLD BOTTLES. n.p., 1981. #MLR9.

Contains item 272.

1302. ———. ONE WIFE; GOLDEN SEEDS; TYPEWRITER QUEENS; COME ON MA; THE GODDESSES. n.p., 1981. #MLR45.

Contains items 279, 284, 321 and 254.

1303. ———. OUR GOAL: WORLD CONQUEST. PART 1. n.p., 1981. #QB4.

1304. ———. OUR GOAL: WORLD CONQUEST. PART 2. n.p., 1981. #QB5.

1305. ———. OUR SHEPHERD: MOSES DAVID. n.p., 1981. #QB8.

Contains item 456.

1306. ———. PAPER POWER. n.p., 1981. #MLR10.

Contains item 345.

1307. ———. THE PHEONIX. Toulouse Cedex, France: Wild Wind Tapes, 1981. #MC7.

Contains item 309.

1308. ———. THE PRINCE OF THE COVENANT: THE FACTS ABOUT THE ANTI-CHRIST. Toulouse Cedex, France: Wild Wind Tapes, 1981. #MC24.

Contains item 816.

1309. ———. THE PSALMS OF DAVID. Toulouse Cedex, France: Wild Wind Tapes, 1981. #MC23.

1310. ———. REVOLUTIONARY LOVEMAKING. Toulouse Cedex, France: Wild Wind Tapes, 1981. #MC13.

Contains item 289.

1311. ——. REVOLUTIONARY SEX. n.p., 1981. #MLR23.

Contains item 288.

1312. ——. REVOLUTIONARY WOMEN. n.p., 1981. #MLR41.

Contains item 280.

1313. ——. RICHMAN, POORMAN; A CHILD'S STORY OF BLOBS; HEAVENLY HOMES. n.p., 1981. #MLR27.

Contains items 390 and 377.

1314. ——. ROUND ROUND ROOM; JAPANESE-SOUTH AMERICAN DREAM. n.p., 1981. #MLR32.

Contains items 397 and 398.

1315. ——. THE 7 WAYS TO KNOW GOD'S WILL; GOD OR MAMMON? Toulouse Cedex, France: Wild Wind Tapes, 1981. #MC25.

Contains item 870.

1316. ——. SEX WORKS. n.p., 1981. #MLR36.

Contains item 348.

1317. ——. SHEPHERD TIME STORY; HOLY HOLES. n.p., 1981. #MLR40.

Contains items 137 and 267.

1318. ——. SHINERS OR SHAMERS?; WONDER WORKING WORDS; REVOLUTIONARY RULES. n.p., 1981. #MLR8.

Contains items 271, 236 and 19.

1319. ——. SMOKING, DRIVING THE TRUCK & THE EXPLOSION. n.p., 1981. #MCC3.

1320. ——. SNOWMAN; HEIDI. n.p., 1981. #MLR16.

Contains items 224 and 235.

1321. ——. SO YOU WANT TO BE A LEADER?; I GOTTA SPLIT 1; I GOTTA SPLIT 2. n.p., 1981. #MLR7.

Contains items 50, 47 and 48.

1322. ——. SPACE CITY; ULTIMATE TRIP. n.p., 1981. #MLR19.

Contains items 99 and 104.

1323. ——. SPACEMEN; IDOLSMASHERS. Toulouse Cedex, France: Wild Wind Tapes, 1981. #MC20.

Contains item 575.

1324.   ——. SPIRIT TREE; DON QUIXOTE; MY LOVE IS A LEGEND; SOUNDS IN THE NIGHT. n.p., 1981. #MLR15.

Contains items 223, 227, 108 and 109.

1325.   ——. THE SPIRIT WORLD. n.p., 1981. #QB9.

Contains item 639.

1326.   ——. SPIRITUAL COMMUNICATIONS; PRAYER POWER. n.p., 1981. #MLR39.

Contains items 446 and 340.

1327.   ——. STAND IN THE GAP; HE STANDS IN THE GAP; A HEAVENLY VISITOR. n.p., 1981. #MLR42.

Contains items 92, 96 and 94.

1328.   ——. STOP, LOOK AND LISTEN. n.p., 1981. #MLR2.

Contains item 97.

1329.   ——. THE STORY OF CASTRO THE REBEL. n.p., 1981. #MCC8.

1330.   ——. TOM THE GANGSTER. n.p., 1981. #MCC7.

1331.   ——. THE TREE; BYE BYE BIRDIE; CITY OF BURIED TREASURE. n.p., 1981. #MLR35.

Contains items 388, 261 and 394.

1332.   ——. WAR AND PEACE; ASK ANY COMMUNIST. n.p., 1981. #MLR29.

Contains items 285 and 286.

1333.   ——. WHAT IS THAT IN THINE HAND?; NEW BOTTLES. n.p., 1981. #MLR48.

Contains items 373 and 281.

1334.   ——. WHO ARE THE REBELS?; LETTER TO A LOVED ONE; NO NEUTRALS; SOCK IT TO ME. n.p., 1981. #MLR13.

Contains items 5, 7 and 51.

1335.   ——. WHY WE MUST DROP OUT. n.p., 1981. #QB3.

1336.   ——. THE WITNESSING REVOLUTION. Toulouse Cedex, France: Wild Wind Tapes, 1981. #MC11.

1337.   ——. THE WORLD TODAY AND TOMORROW. PART 1. n.p., 1981. #QB6.

1338. ------. THE WORLD TODAY AND TOMORROW. PART 2. n.p., 1981. #QB7.

1339. ------. YOUR SPIRITUAL LIFE & WALK WITH THE LORD. n.p., 1981. #QB2.

1340. Berg, Virginia Brandt (Grandmother). BACA; BOOMERANG; PRECIOUS PROMISES; APPROPRIATING FAITH; LOVE FOR OTHERS; STAND OUT FOR JESUS. n.p., 1981. #MM1.

1341. ------. BE STILL; IT'S SO BECAUSE GOD SAID SO; THE STRENGTH OF WEAKNESS; HOLD ON A LITTLE LONGER; THE STANDARD; THE RECREATION MIRACLE; WHO SINNED? n.p., 1981. #MM2

1342. ------. BRING BACK THE ARK; HAPPINESS; CLEANSING; THE STRONGBOX; THE SEAT OF THE SCORNFUL; FIXED DETERMINATION. n.p., 1981. #MM18.

1343. ------. BROKEN THINGS; CLOSER WALK; HUMILITY; CONFESSION; TODAY; WHAT IS HEALING? n.p., 1981. #MM8.

1344. ------. DIVINE EXCHANGE; EXTRA ALLOWANCE; DINING ALONE TONIGHT; LONLINESS; INFLUENCE--ACTS 5; THE WILL OF GOD IN HEALING. n.p., 1981. #MM17.

1345. ------. DOUBTS & HOW TO GET RID OF THEM; SECRET PLACE; COMPROMISE & CONFORMITY; WILL OF GOD NOT HARD; WAIT FOR THE LIGHT; GOD'S FAITHFULNESS. n.p., 1981. #MM3.

1346. ------. ENCOURAGEMENT; GOD'S WILL; SECRET PLACE-- TEMPTATION; GOD DOES HEAL TODAY; PROMISES OF GOD; FAITH & WILL OF GOD; PUT UP THY SWORD. n.p., 1981. #MM7.

1347. ------. FORGETTING THE PAST; SENSE OF VALUES; JUST A CLOSER WALK; THE BREAD OF LIFE; TRANSFORMED; DARE TO STAND ALONE. n.p., 1981. #MM4.

1348. ------. GOD'S CURE FOR LONELINESS; REAPING; WINGS; GREAT FAITH; IF I GAINED THE WORLD. n.p., 1981. #MM15.

1349. ------. GUIDANCE; THE COMMON PLACE; RECEIVE; PERSONAL CONVERSATION WITH CHRIST; HE SATISFIES COMPLETELY. n.p., 1981. #MM12.

1350. ------. HEBREWS 12--HEALING; BLACK OUT; DISAPPOINTMENTS; HEALING GLORIFIES GOD; LET IT PASS; SWEET HOUR OF PRAYER. n.p., 1981. #MM13.

1351. ------. THE LADDER OF FAITH; MOSES LEFT EGYPT BEHIND; FAITHFULNESS OF GOD; DANIEL; THE TONGUE; GOD'S INTOLERABLE COMPLIMENT. n.p., 1981. #MM6.

1352. ------. MEDITATION MOMENTS. Toulouse Cedex, France: Wild Wind Tapes, n.d. 10 Tapes.

1353.   ——. MEET GOD'S CONDITIONS; GREATER VICTORIES OUT OF
         SEEMING DEFEATS; ROMANS 8:11; WHEN GOD SPEAKS; THE
         TONGUE; THE SECRET PLACE. n.p., 1981. #MM5.

1354.   ——. POWER IN THAT NAME; OUT OF THE DEPTHS; THE TONGUE;
         OUR PERSONAL RESPONSIBILITIES; AFTERWARD (HEBREWS 12);
         BITTERNESS & VENGEANCE. n.p., 1981. #MM21.

1355.   ——. PROMISES; 'GOOD PEOPLE' OR BORN AGAIN CHRISTIANS;
         VICTORY FROM SEEMING DEFEAT; LITTLE PEOPLE (SECOND
         FIDDLE); THE UNCHANGING CHRIST. n.p., 1981. #MM19.

1356.   ——. SELF LIFE; CHRIST IN YOU—COL. 3; FIVE MINUTES;
         PROMISES OF GOD; WEAKNESS VS. STRENGTH; ALL THINGS OR
         ONE THING. n.p., 1981. #MM14.

1357.   ——. THE SHUT-INS; POWER OF POSITIVE SPEAKING; MEASURE
         OF FAITH; ROYAL ROAD TO HAPPINESS; CITIZENSHIP; UNBELIEF.
         n.p., 1981. #MM10.

1358.   ——. TAKE JESUS AS YOUR SAVIOR; YESTERDAY; IN THE
         GARDEN; OLD AGE & VICTORY; IMPORTUNITY; TRANSFORMED.
         n.p., 1981. #MM11.

1359.   ——. THOUGHTS; ASSURANCE OF THINGS HOPED FOR; A SONG IN
         THE HEART; JUDGE NOT (CRITICAL TONGUE); WEAKNESS VS.
         STRENGTH; THE MIRACULOUS. n.p., 1981. #MM20.

1360.   ——. WINGS; COMPOSE & REPOSE; OPEN MY EYES THAT I MAY
         SEE; THE UNCONTROLLED TONGUE; ALL THINGS OR ONE THING;
         MANSIONS. n.p., 1981. #MM22.

1361.   ——. WINGS; WORTHINESS; SECRET PLACE—RENEWING; SELF-
         PITY & DEPRESSION; PRAISE & THANKSGIVING; PSALM 27—
         TESTIMONY. n.p., 1981. #MM9.

1362.   ——. WINGS (NO. 2); HUMILITY; UTTERLY DESTROY; GLORIFIED
         SAVIOR; BIRTHDAY SERVICE; THE TRUE CHRISTMAS. n.p., 1981.
         #MM16.

1363.   The Children Of God. AARON. n.p.: Music That Made The Revolution,
         n.d. #SC1.

1364.   ——. ACTS TAPE 1. n.p., 1981. #SC8.

1365.   ——. ACTS TAPE 2. n.p., 1981. #SC9.

1366.   ——. ASK HIM IN YOUR HEART. n.p.: Thank COG Song Tapes, n.d.
         #TCC3.

1367.   ——. THE BAND FROM LA—LA BAND. n.p., n.d. #ST21.

1368.   ——. BIBLE STORIES AND OTHERS IN SONG ESPECIALLY
         RECORDED FOR CHILDREN. Toulouse Cedex, France: Wild Wind
         Tapes, n.d.

1369. ——. CHILDREN'S MO LETTERS WITH SOUND EFFECTS READ BY BARUCH SCRIBE. Toulouse Cedex, France: Wild Wind Tapes, 1981. #WWC3.

1370. ——. I CORINTHIANS 7-II CORINTHIANS. n.p., 1981. #SC11.

1371. ——. EXODUS 1-15. n.p., 1981. #SC24.

1372. ——. EXODUS 16-31. n.p., 1981. #SC25.

1373. ——. EXODUS 32-40. n.p., 1981. #SC26.

1374. ——. FEED MY LAMBS MEMORY VERSES; IN SONG WITH STEPHEN SHEEP. Toulouse Cedex, France: Wild Wind Tapes, 1981. #WWC11.

1375. ——. GALATIONS-COLOSSIANS. n.p., 1981. #SC12.

1376. ——. GENESIS 1-20. n.p., 1981. #SC21.

1377. ——. GENESIS 21-34. n.p., 1981. #SC22.

1378. ——. GENESIS 35-50. n.p., 1981. #SC23.

1379. ——. HEAVENLY HOMES WITH NICHOLAS ROBINHOOD & SOUNDS IN THE NIGHT READ BY URIAH THE HITTITE. Toulouse Cedex, France: Wild Wind Tapes, 1981. #WWC5.

1380. ——. HOW LONG YOU BEEN WAITING? n.p.: Thank COG Song Tapes, n.d. #TCC1.

1381. ——. JAMES-JUDE. n.p., 1981. #SC14.

1382. ——. JOHN TAPE 1. n.p., 1981. #SC6.

1383. ——. JOHN TAPE 2. n.p., 1981. #SC7.

1384. ——. KING DAVID OPERA—BEN & RUTH. n.p., n.d. #ST22.

1385. ——. LET NOT YOUR HEART BE TROUBLED. n.p.: Thank COG Song Tapes, n.d. #TCC4.

1386. ——. LUKE TAPE 1. n.p., 1981. #SC4.

1387. ——. LUKE TAPE 2. n.p., 1981. #SC5.

1388. ——. MARK. n.p., 1981. #SC3.

1389. ——. MATTHEW TAPE 1. n.p., 1981. #SC1.

1390. ——. MATTHEW TAPE 2. n.p., 1981. #SC2.

1391. ——. MOVEMENTS—MUSIC & SONG TAPE. Firenze, Italy: Pisces Tapes, n.d.

1392. ——. MOUNTAIN MEN; HEBREWS 11. n.p.: Music That Made The Revolution, n.d. #SC4.

1393. ——. THE MUSIC THAT MADE THE REVOLUTION. n.p., n.d. #SC8 (4 tapes).

1394. ——. MUSIC WITH MEANING CASSETTE TAPES. n.p., n.d.

1395. ——. NICE TO BE HERE—LA BAND. n.p., n.d. #ST19.

1396. ——. PROVERBS 1-25. n.p., 1981. #SC19.

1397. ——. PROVERBS 25-SONG OF SOLOMON. n.p., 1981. #SC20.

1398. ——. THE PSALMS IN SONG. Toulouse Cedex, France: Wild Wind Tapes, 1981. #WWS12.

1399. ——. PSALMS TAPE 1. n.p., 1981. #SC16.

1400. ——. PSALMS TAPE 2. n.p., 1981. #SC17.

1401. ——. PSALMS TAPE 3. n.p., 1981. #SC18.

1402. ——. QUOTES FROM GRANDPA READ BY ELIAS BURNFREE. Toulouse Cedex, France: Wild Wind Tapes, 1981. #WWC8.

1403. ——. ROMANS-I CORINTHIANS 6. n.p., 1981. #SC10.

1404. ——. REVELATION. n.p., 1981. #SC15.

1405. ——. SET CARD—ABRAHAM. n.p.: Scripture Tapes, #SCC1 (2 tapes).

1406. ——. THE SET CARD IN SONG, SETS 1-8. Toulouse Cedex, France: Wild Wind Tapes, 1981. #WWC4.

1407. ——. SHADRACH, MESHACK, ABEDNEGO AND OTHERS. Toulouse Cedex, France: Wild Wind Tapes, n.d.

1408. ——. 'SPACE CITY' AND SONGS—AARON. n.p., n.d. #CLC2.

1409. ——. THE STORY OF LOVE TAPE 1. Zurich: World Services, 1981. #SL1.

1410. ——. THE STORY OF LOVE TAPE 2. Zurich: World Services, 1981. #SL2.

1411. ——. THE STORY OF LOVE TAPE 3. Zurich: World Services, 1981. #SL3.

1412. ——. THE STORY OF LOVE TAPE 4. Zurich: World Services, 1981. #SL4.

1413. ——. TENDER LOVING CARE.—MUSIC TAPE. Toulouse Cedex, France: Wild Wind Tapes, n.d.

1414. ——. THESSALONIANS-HEBREWS. n.p., 1981. #SC13.

1415. ——. WATCH A BABY DIE—LA BAND. n.p., n.d. #ST20.

1416. ———. THE WITNESSING SETS READ BY ELIAS BURNFREE. Toulouse Cedex, France: Wild Wind Tapes, 1981. #WWC9.

1417. ———. YOU GOTTA BE A BABY! n.p.: Thank COG Song Tapes, n.d. #TCC2.

III

SECONDARY MATERIAL

A. SCHOLARLY MATERIAL

The scholarly articles, by and large, attempt to describe and explain the COG and its practices from an objective point of view. If criticisms are made of certain features of the group, praise is often given to other features as well.

1418. Anthony, Dick and Thomas Robbins. "New Religions, Families and 'Brainwashing.'" IN GOD WE TRUST. Edited by Thomas Robbins and Dick Anthony. New Brunswick: Transaction Books, 1981. pp. 264, 269, 271.

1419. Barker, Eileen. "Free to Choose?" Mimeographed. n.p., n.d. pp. 3, 5-6.

1420. Beckford, James A. "Explaining Religious Movements." INTERNATIONAL SOCIAL SCIENCE JOURNAL, 24 (1977) 240.

1421. Brown, Marvin. "Some Responses to the 'New Religions' in West Germany." Mimeographed, 1979. pp. 2, 3.

1422. ------. "Germany and the New Religions." NEW RELIGIOUS MOVEMENTS NEWSLETTER, 1 (December) 2, 13.

1423. Carroll, Jackson W. "Transcendence and Mystery in the Counter-Culture." RELIGION IN LIFE, 42 (1973) 361, 363, 369, 371.

1424. Cohen, Daniel. "The Children of God." THE NEW BELIEVERS: YOUNG RELIGION IN AMERICA. New York: M. Evans and Co., 1975. pp. 21-40.

1425. Colton, Joel. Introduction to NEW RELIGIOUS MOVEMENTS IN AMERICA. Edited by George Baker, Jacob Needleman and Peter Payne. New York: The Rockefeller Foundation, September 1979. p. 4.

1426. Dart, John. "New Religious Movement and American Society." NEW RELIGIOUS MOVEMENTS IN AMERICA. Edited by George Baker, Jacob Needleman and Peter Payne. New York: The Rockefeller Foundation, September 1979. p. 9.

1427. Davis, Rex and James T. Richardson. "A More Honest and Objective Look at the Children of God." Paper presented at the Society for the Scientific Study of Religion annual meeting, October 1975, in Milwaukee. Mimeographed.

1428. ------. "The Organization and Functioning of the Children of God."
       SOCIOLOGICAL ANALYSIS, 37 (1976) 321-94.

1429. Delgado, Richard. "Limits to Proselytizing." SOCIETY, 17 (March-April
       1980) 25, 30, 31, 33.

1430. Doress, Irvin and Jack Nusan Porter. "Kids in Cults." SOCIETY, 15
       (May-June 1978) 70.

       Also published as — "Kids in Cults: Why They Join, Why They Stay, Why
       They Leave." Brookline, MA: Reconciliation Associates, January
       1979:1,3,17.

       Also published as — "Kids in Cults." IN GODS WE TRUST. Edited by
       Thomas Robbins and Dick Anthony. New Brunswick, NJ: Transaction
       Books, 1981. p. 299.

1431. Ellwood, Robert S., Jr. "Communes and the Children of God." ONE
       WAY: THE JESUS MOVEMENT AND ITS MEANING. Englewood Cliffs,
       NJ: Prentice-Hall, 1973, pp. 101-11.

1432. Enroth, Ronald M., Edward E. Ericson, Jr. and C. Breckinridge Peters.
       "The Doom-Saying Exclusivists: Hell? No, We Won't Go." THE JESUS
       PEOPLE: OLD-TIME RELIGION IN THE AGE OF ACQUARIOUS.
       Grand Rapids: William B. Eerdmans, 1972. pp. 21-54.

       Also published in an British version as — THE STORY OF THE JESUS
       PEOPLE: A FACTUAL SURVEY. Exeter: The Paternoster Press, 1972.

1433. Fairfield, Richard, ed. UTOPIA, U.S.A. San Francisco: Alternatives
       Foundation, 1972. p. 56.

1434. Flinn, Frank K. "Book Review—'The Social Impact of New Religious
       Movements.' Edited by Bryan Wilson." ALLIANCE FOR THE
       PRESERVATION OF RELIGIOUS LIBERTY NEWSLETTER, October
       1981. p. 4.

1435. Foss, Daniel A. and Ralph W. Larkin. "The Roar of the Lemming: Youth
       Postmovement Groups, and the Life Construction Crisis." RELIGIOUS
       CHANGE AND CONTINUITY. Edited by Harry M. Johnson. San
       Francisco: Jossey-Bass, 1979. pp. 264, 268, 269, 271.

1436. Fried, Eric B. "The New Religious Movements in Contemporary
       America." Mimeographed. Cambridge, MA: Harvard College, March
       1980. pp. 7, 20, 130, 132.

1437. Gann, L.H. "New Book About Contemporary Religious Scene—Thomas
       Robins and Dick Anthony, eds. 'In Gods We Trust: New Patterns of
       Religious   Pluralism   in   America.'" ALLIANCE   FOR   THE
       PRESERVATION OF RELIGIOUS LIBERTY NEWSLETTER, July 1981.
       p. 3.

1438. Gardner, Hugh. "The Destiny and Legacy of the Modern Commune
       Movement." THE CHILDREN OF PROSPERITY: THIRTEEN MODERN

AMERICAN COMMUNES. New York: St. Martin's Press, 1978. pp. 247-48.

1439. Gaustad, Edwin Scott. DISSENT IN AMERICAN RELIGION. Chicago: University of Chicago, 1973. p. 147.

1440. Hall, John R. THE WAYS OUT: UTOPIAN COMMUNAL GROUPS IN AN AGE OF BABYLON. London: Routledge & Kegan Paul, 1978. p. 104

1441. Haack, Friederich W. "New Youth Religions, Psychomutation and Technological Civilization." INTERNATIONAL REVIEW OF MISSION, 67 (October 1978) 436-47.

1442. Hargrove, Barbara. "Evil Eyes and Religious Choices." SOCIETY, 17 (March-April 1980) 20.

1443. ------. THE SOCIOLOGY OF RELIGION: CLASSICAL AND CONTEMPORARY APPROACHES. Arlington Heights, IL: AHM Publishing Corporation, 1979. pp. 298, 304-06.

1444. Henderson, C. William. AWAKENING. Englewood Cliffs, NJ: Prentice-Hall, 1975. p. 220.

1445. Hudson, Winthrop S. "The Jesus Cult." RELIGION IN AMERICA. New York: Charles Scribner's Sons, 1965. pp. 431-33.

1446. Hyde, Margaret O. BRAINWASHING AND OTHER FORMS OF MIND CONTROL. New York: McGraw-Hill, 1977. pp. 119-20.

1447. Kirschner Associates, Inc. and the Institute for the Study of American Religion. "Children of God." RELIGIOUS REQUIREMENTS AND PRACTICES OF CERTAIN SELECTED GROUPS: A HANDBOOK FOR CHAPLAINS. Baltimore: Headquarters, Department of the Army, April 1978. pp. I 11-16.

1448. Leech, Kenneth. "Jesus Revolution." YOUTH QUAKE: THE GROWTH OF A COUNTER-CULTURE THROUGH TWO DECADES. Totowa, NJ: Littlefield, Adams & Co., 1977. pp. 155-57, 159, 165.

1449. Leming, Michael R. and Ted C. Smith. "The Children of God as a Social Movement." Paper presented at the annual meeting of the Pacific Sociological Association, 1973, in Scottsdale, AZ. Mimeographed.

1450. Le Moult, John E. "Kidnapping Members of Religious Groups--'Deprogrammers.'" Memorandum to Privacy Committee, American Civil Liberties Union, 1 December 1976. p. 5.

1451. Lindsey, Jonathan A. CHANGE AND CHALLENGE. Wilmington, NC: McGrath, 1977. pp. 101-02.

1452. Maher, Frederick. "Mind Control and Religious Liberty." Paper presented at the annual meeting of the Society for the Scientific Study of Religion, 1967, in Chicago. Mimeographed. p. 14.

1453.   Melton, J. Gordon with James V. Geisendorfer. A DIRECTORY OF RELIGIOUS BODIES IN THE UNITED STATES. New York: Garland, 1977. pp. 101, 277.

1454.   Melton, J. Gordon. THE ENCYCLOPEDIA OF AMERICAN RELIGIONS. Vol. I. Wilmington, NC: McGrath, 1978. p. xi.

1455.   ———. THE ENCYCLOPEDIA OF AMERICAN RELIGIONS. VOL. II. Wilmington, NC: McGrath, 1978. pp. 447, 452-54, 538.

1456.   Melville, Keith. COMMUNES IN THE COUNTER CULTURE. New York: William Morrow, 1972. pp. 210, 212.

1457.   Persson, Bertil, Bjorn Sahlin and Ted A Nordquist. "New Religions in Europe: What Is Happening in West Germany?" n.p., n.d. pp. 2, 9.

1458.   Peterson, D.W. and A.L. Mauss. "The Cross and the Commune: An Interpretation of the Jesus People." RELIGION IN SOCIOLOGICAL PERSPECTIVE. Edited by Charles Y. Glock. Belmont, CA: Wadsworth, 1973. pp. 265, 274-75.

1459.   Prichard, Anne. "'DEPROGRAMMING:' A BOOK OF DOCUMENTS." New York: American Civil Liberties Union, 1977. pp. 3, 11, 35, 154.

1460.   Pritchett, W. Douglas. "The Role of Charisma in the Evolution of New Religious Groups." Master's thesis, University of Houston, 1980. 132 pp.

1461.   Richardson, James T. "The Jesus Movement Outside America." Mimeographed. Reno: University of Nevada, Spring 1976. 19 pp.

1462.   ———. "Brainwashing." SOCIETY, 17 (March-April 1980) 19.

1463.   Robbins, Thomas and Dick Anthony. "New Religions, Families, and Brainwashing." SOCIETY, 15 (May-June 1978) 78, 80, 82.

1464.   ———. "'Cults' vs. 'Shrinks': Psychiatry and the Control of Religious Movements." Paper presented to The Association for the Sociology of Religion, 1979. p. 13.

1465.   Robbins, Thomas, Dick Anthony and Thomas Curtis. "Youth Culture Religious Movements: Evaluating the Integrative Hypothesis." SOCIOLOGICAL QUARTERLY, 16 (Winter 1975) 48-64.

1466.   Shupe, Anson D. "Cults of Anti-Cultism." SOCIETY, 17 (March-April 1980) 43-46.

1467.   Shupe, Anson D., Jr. and David G. Bromley. THE NEW VIGILANTES: DEPROGRAMMERS, ANTI-CULTISTS, AND THE NEW RELIGIONS. Beverly Hills: Sage Publications, 1980.

1468.   Singer, Margaret Thaler. "Coming out of cults." PSYCHOLOGY TODAY, 12 (January 1979) 72-80, 82.

1469.   Slade, Margot. "New Religious Groups: Membership and Legal Battles." PSYCHOLOGY TODAY, 12 (January 1979) 81.

1470. Veysey, Laurence. THE COMMUNAL EXPERIENCE: ANARCHIST AND MYSTICAL COUNTER-CULTURES IN AMERICA. New York: Harper & Row, 1973: 65, 411-13, 458, 459, 470.

1471. Wagner, Frederick Norman. "'The Children of God.' A Theological and Historical Assessment of the Jesus People Phenomenon." Doctor of Ministry thesis, Fuller Theological Seminary, 1971. pp. 119-125.

1472. Wallis, Roy. "Charisma, Commitment and Control in a New Religious Movement." Mimeographed. Belfast: The Queen's University of Belfast, February 1981. 42 pp.

1473. ------. GOD'S NEW NATION. Forthcoming.

1474. ------. "Millennialism and community: Observations on the Children of God" and "Sex, Marriage and the Children of God." SALVATION AND PROTEST: STUDIES OF SOCIAL AND RELIGIOUS MOVEMENTS. New York: St. Martin's Press, 1979. pp. 51-90.

1475. ------. NEW RELIGIOUS MOVEMENTS NEWSLETTER, 1 (March 1979) 11.

1476. ------. "Observation on the Children of God." The Sociological Review, 24 (November 1976) 807-29.

1477. ------. "The Rebirth of the God?: Reflections on the New Religions in the West." An Inaugural Lecture delivered before The Queen's University of Belfast, 3 May 1978, in Belfast. Mimeographed. pp. 5-7, 12, 15, 20, 23.

1478. ------. "Recruiting Christian Manpower." SOCIETY, 15 (May-June 1978) 72-74.

1479. ------. "Yesterday's Children: Structural and Cultural Change in a New Religious Movement." THE SOCIAL IMPACT OF NEW RELIGIOUS MOVEMENTS. Edited by Bryan Wilson. New York: The Rose of Sharon Press, 1981. pp. 97-133.

1480. Wuthnow, Robert. THE CONSCIOUSNESS REFORMATION. Berkeley: University of California Press, 1976. pp. 34-36.

1481. ------. "Political Aspects of the Quietistic Revival." IN GODS WE TRUST. Edited by Thomas Robbins and Dick Anthony. New Brunswick, NJ: Transwick Books, 1981. pp. 232-34.

B. RELIGIOUS PUBLICATIONS

Articles on the COG in religious publications tend to be critical, but unlike the anti-COG articles in section F, they generally try to provide descriptive material on the group, its development, etc. These articles are not, by and large, as analytical as the scholarly ones in section A, however.

1482. The Baptist Messenger. "Children of God Are Moving." THE BAPTIST MESSENGER, 61 (5 October 1972) 2.

1483. Barker, Eileen. "Some Thoughts on the Unification Church and Other New Religious Movements." CLERGY REVIEW, September 1980. p. 3.

1484. Campus Ministry Communications. NEW MESSIAHS ATTRACT YOUTH. Chicago: Lutheran Council in the USA, 1977. pp. 1-2.

1485. Challenge. "The Children of God." CHALLENGE (New Zealand), 16 December 1972. pp. 6-7.

1486. ------. "Far out Group Causes Strife." CHALLENGE (New Zealand), 19 February 1972. p. 9

1487. ------. "Inquiry into Children of God Movement Waged." CHALLENGE (New Zealand), 20 January 1973. p 7.

1488. Christ for the Nations. "The Day God's Children Died." CHRIST FOR THE NATIONS, July 1975. pp. 12-13.

1489. Christian Inquirer. "N.Y. Attorney General Condemns Children of God." CHRISTIAN INQUIRER, 8 November 1974. p. 8.

1490. Christianity Today. "Children, Go Home: Will Members of the Children of God Be Coming Home Soon?" CHRISTIANITY TODAY, 12 August 1977. pp. 33-34.

1491. ------. "The Children of God." CHRISTIANITY TODAY, 5 November 1971. p. 3.

1492. ------. "The Children of God: Disciples of Deception." Washington D.C.: CHRISTIANITY TODAY, 1977. 5 pp.

1493. ------. "False Prophecy?" CHRISTIANITY TODAY, 15 February 1974. p. 49.

1494. ------. "Home For Christmas?" CHRISTIANITY TODAY, 17 December 1971. p. 35.

1495.   ——. "From Jonah to Jeremiah." CHRISTIANITY TODAY, 25 September 1970. pp. 24-25.

1496.   ——. "Religion in Transit." CHRISTIANITY TODAY, 13 January 1978. p. 53.

1497.   ——. "Religion in Transit." CHRISTIANITY TODAY, 5 May 1978, p. 53

1498.   Cornerstone. "COG Album." CORNERSTONE, 8 (1980) 44.

1499.   ——. "COG Update." CORNERSTONE, 8 (1979) 22, 24.

1500.   ——. "A Peek Inside the COG." CORNERSTONE, 6 (1978) 10.

1501.   Corry, Geoffrey. 'PHASE 2—THE CHILDREN OF GOD ARRIVE,' AND 'EXPOSURE AND COUNTER-ATTACK.' JESUS REVOLUTION: THE GROWTH OF JESUS COMMUNES IN BRITAIN AND IRELAND. London: British Council of Churches Youth Dept., 1973. pp. 18-27.

1502.   Davies, Horton. CHRISTIAN DEVIATIONS: THE CHALLENGE OF THE NEW SPIRITUAL MOVEMENTS. Philadelphia: The Westminster Press, 1972. p. 17.

1503.   Davis, Rex. "All Things in Common." RISK. Zurich: World Council of Churches, 1973.

1504.   ——. "Lift Up Your Hearts." RISK. Zurich: World Council of Churches, 1976.

1505.   ——. "Locusts and Wild Honey." ISBN No. 2825405965. Zurich: World Council of Churches, 1978. 123 pp.

1506.   ——. "Where Have All the Children Gone?" Forthcoming in a book edited by E. Barker, L.S.E.

1507.   Drakeford, John W. CHILDREN OF DOOM: A SOBERING LOOK AT THE COMMUNE MOVEMENT. Nashville: Broadman Press, 1972.

1508.   Enroth, Ronald M. "A Catalog of Cults." THE CHRISTIAN READER, November-December 1980. pp. 43-54.

        Excerpted from item 1510.

1509.   ——. "The Children of God." YOUTH, BRAINWASHING, AND THE EXTREMIST CULTS. Grand Rapids: Zondervan, 1977. pp. 35-65.

1510.   ——. THE LURE OF THE CULTS. Chappaqua, NY: Christian Herald Books, 1979. pp. 26-27, 51, 84-86, 94.

1511.   ——. "The Seduction of the Searchers." EVANGELICAL NEWSLETTER, Philadelphia, n.d. 1 p.

1512.   ——. "A Primer on the Major 'New Age' Cults." EVANGELICAL NEWSLETTER, Philadelphia, n.d. 1 p.

1513. Ericson, Edward E., Jr. and Paul MacPherson. "The Deceptions of the Children of God." CHRISTIANITY TODAY, 20 July 1973. pp. 14, 15, 18, 20.

1514. ------. "Are the Children of God Brainwashed?" CHRISTIAN HERALD, October 1973. pp. 32-40.

1515. Fiske, Edward B. "Children of God: For Better ... or Worse." Christian Herald, 95 (July 1972) 12-13, 16-17, 19.

1516. Garvey, John, ed. ALL OUR SONS AND DAUGHTERS. Springfield, IL: Templegate, n.d. pp. 7-9.

1517. Gray Gordon. "With the Children of God in Amsterdam." THE PRESBYTERIAN HERALD, 1972. p. 13.

1518. Hefley, James C. "Mo's Storm Troopers." THE YOUTHNAPPERS. Wheaton, IL: Victor Books, 1977. pp. 128-47.

1519. Hollenweger, Walter J. "When Young People Convert." INTERNATIONAL REVIEW OF MISSION, 67 (October 1978) 459-60.

1520. Hopkins, Joseph M. "Baiting the Hook." CHRISTIANITY TODAY, 30 December 1977. pp. 40-41.

1521. ------. "The Children of God: Disciples of Deception." CHRISTIANITY TODAY, 18 February 1977. pp. 18-23.

1522. ------. "The Children of God: Fewer and Far Out." CHRISTIANITY TODAY, 25 January 1980. pp. 40-41.

1523. ------. "Children of God: New Revelations." CHRISTIANITY TODAY, 24 February 1978. p. 44.

1524. ------. "Children of God--Update." NEW RELIGIOUS MOVEMENTS UPDATE, 4 (December 1980) 42-45.

1525. ------. "Keeping Up with the New Cults." EVANGELICAL NEWSLETTER, 7 (7 March 1980) 4.

1526. Hunt, Dave. THE CULT EXPLOSION. Irvine, CA: Harvest House Publishers, 1980. pp. 85, 86, 151.

1527. Jacob, Michael. POP GOES JESUS: AN INVESTIGATION OF POP RELIGION IN BRITAIN AND AMERICA. London: Mowbrays, 1972. pp. 21-24, 35, 37.

1528. Jorstad, Erling. "The Children of God: A Commune That Failed." THAT NEW TIME RELIGION: THE JESUS REVIVAL IN AMERICA. Minneapolis: Augsburg Publishing House, 1972: 104-11, 123, 125.

1529. Kelly, Dean M. "De-Programming: What's Going on Here?" Mimeographed. New York: National Council of Churches. pp. 1, 8.

1530. Knight, Walter L. "Communes for Christ." JESUS PEOPLE COME ALIVE. Wheaton, IL: Tyndale House, 1971. pp. 41-49.

1531. Langford, Harris. "The Children of God: Offspring of Deceit." TRAPS:
       A PROBE OF THOSE STRANGE NEW CULTS. Decatur, GA:
       Presbyterian Church in America, 1977. pp. 23-42.

1532. Larsen, David L. "Aberations Evangelicals Face: 'The Children of God.'"
       THE DISCERNER, 8 (October-December 1975) 4-6.

1533. Lochhaas, Philip H. HOW TO RESPOND TO ... THE NEW CHRISTIAN
       RELIGIONS. Saint Louis: Concordia, 1979. pp. 17-19.

1534. McBeth, Leon. "Children of God: Storm Troopers of the Jesus
       Movement." STRANGE NEW RELIGIONS. Nashville: Broadman Press,
       1977. pp. 63-78.

1535. MacCollam, Joel A. A CARNIVAL OF SOULS: RELIGIOUS CULTS AND
       YOUNG PEOPLE. New York: Seabury, 1979. pp. 168-77.

1536. McFadden, Michael. "The Children of God." THE JESUS REVOLUTION.
       New York: Harrow Books, 1972. pp. 84-98.

1537. McFarland, Norma. "I Lost My Daughter to a Cult." CHRISTIAN
       CRUSADE WEEKLY, 14 (1 December 1974) 2.

1538. Marty, Martin E. "The Comet That Fizzled." THE CHRISTIAN
       CENTURY, 27 February 1974. p. 247.

1539. Melton, J. Gordon. "Comet Kohoutek: Fizzle of the Century." FATE, 27
       (May 1974) 58-64.

1540. O'Brien, Robert. "The Children of God: The Jesus Movement Spawns a
       Radical New Denomination." HOME MISSIONS, December 1971. pp. 25-
       37.

1541. Oosterwal, Gottfried. "The Children of God." NEW RELIGIOUS
       MOVEMENTS UP-DATE, 3 (July 1979) 35-44.

1542. Peterson, William J. "The Children of God: Walled-In Zealots."
       ETERNITY, 23 (September 1972) 40-42.

1543. Plowman, Edward E. The Jesus Movement in America. Elgin, IL: David
       C. Cook, 1971. pp. 59-61.

1544. ——. "'Straights' Meet 'Streets.'" CHRISTIANITY TODAY, 29 January
       1971. p. 35.

1545. ——. "Ted Patrick Acquitted: Open Season for Deprogrammers."
       CHRISTIANITY TODAY, 31 August 1973. pp. 40-41.

1546. ——. "WCC Central Committee: Fellowship Adrift." CHRISTIANITY
       TODAY, 15 September 1972. pp. 45, 46.

1547. ——. "Where Are All the Children Now?" CHRISTIANITY TODAY, 27
       April 1973. pp. 35-36.

1548. ――――. "Where Have All the Children Gone?" CHRISTIANITY TODAY, 5 November 1971. pp. 38-40.

1549. Pritchett Ballard. RELIGIOUS CULTS. Minneapolis: Office of Research and Analysis, of the American Lutheran Church, August 1976. p. 2.

1550. Rzepeck, Nestor. "Beware of the Children of God." THE OBSERVER (United Church of Canada), August 1972.

1551. Sailhamer, John. "Children: Soft on Parents." CHRISTIANITY TODAY, 31 August 1973. p 41.

1552. Schaeffer, Edith. "What Witness Will God Give?" CHRISTIANITY TODAY, 21 October 1977. p. 28.

1553. Scheflin, Alan W. and Edward M. Opton, Jr. THE MIND MANIPULATORS. New York: Paddington Press, 1978. pp. 52-61.

1554. Schwartz, Paul. "Young People and the New Religions." THE CHRISTIAN HOME, April 1979.

1555. The Shantyman. "Children of God Not Christian Says a Minister in Yonge Street Strip." THE SHANTYMAN (Ontario), September 1975. p 2.

1556. Short, Shirl. "The Menace of the New Cults." MOODY MONTHLY, 77 (July-August 1977) 1-7.

1557. Sovik, Arne. "A Selected and Annotated Bibliography." INTERNATIONAL REVIEW OF MISSION, 67 (October 1978) p. 476.

1558. Streiker, Lowell. "The Children of God." THE CULTS ARE COMING. Nashville: Abingdon Press, 1978. pp. 50-66.

1559. ――――. THE JESUS TRIP: ADVENT OF THE JESUS FREAKS. Nashville: Abingdon Press, 1971. pp. 50-54.

1560. Texas Methodist. "'Children of God' Deny Charges by Mother in an Alleged Kidnapping Case." TEXAS METHODIST, 17 November 1972.

1561. Voke, Stanley J. "Beware of 'The Children of God.'" LIFE OF FAITH (U.K.), 16 September 1972. p. 12.

1562. Ward, Hiley H. "Apostles of Faith or Fear: Children of God." The Far-Out Saints of the Jesus Communes. New York: Association Press, 1972. pp. 53-73.

1563. Weldon, John. "A Sampling of the New Religions." INTERNATIONAL REVIEW OF MISSION, 67 (October 1978) 413-19.

1564. Wikstrom, Lester. "Happy Hookers for Jesus; Children of God's Sex revolution." NEW RELIGIOUS MOVEMENTS UP-DATE, 1 (December 1977) 59-63.

1565. Willoughby, William F. "'Deprogramming' Jesus Freaks and Others: Can America Tolerate Private Inquisitions?" THE CHRISTIAN CENTURY, 2 May 1973. p. 511.

1566. Zimmerman, Marie. "The Jesus Movement." RIC SUPPLEMENT. Strasburg, France: Cerdic Publications, 1973. pp. 4-5.

C. JOURNALISTIC MATERIAL

Most of the articles written in a journalistic style are critical of the COG and a few are sensationalistic and inflammatory in nature. Those by Roy Wallis (items 3439 and 3440), however, attempt to be merely descriptive. All of the items in this section do share a common trait, an attempt to acquaint the general public with the group, its beliefs and practices.

1567. Alexander, Shana. "A Lust for Leadership." NEWSWEEK, 7 January 1974. p. 29.

1568. The Alliance for the Preservation of Religious Liberty. CONCILIATORY DIALOGUE: A PEACEFUL MEANS TO SAVE THE FAMILY. Los Angeles: Alliance for the Preservation of Religious Liberty, 1977. pp. 3-4.

1569. Americans Preserving Religious Liberty. DEALING WITH SOMEONE WHO HAS JOINED A RELIGIOUS 'CULT:' A GUIDE FOR FAMILY AND FRIENDS. Oakland, CA: APRL, 1982. p. 1.

1570. Bourgoin, Mary Fay. "Cults Attract Ex-Catholics." NATIONAL CATHOLIC REPORTER, 15 (20 April 1979) 1.

1571. Bruning, Fred, Anthony Collings and Carolyn Paul. "Europe's Rising Cults." NEWSWEEK, 7 May 1979. pp. 100, 102.

1572. Conway, Flo and Jim Siegelman. SNAPPING: AMERICA'S EPIDEMIC OF SUDDEN PERSONALITY CHANGE. Philadelphia: J.B. Lippincott, 1978. pp. 15, 28, 63-65, 80-81, 219.

1573. Craig, Mary. "The Jesus Movement in Britain." CATHOLIC GAZETTE, September 1972. pp. 3-7.

1574. Gehr, Betty P. "Letter to the editor." TIME, 14 February 1972. p. 4.

1575. Harris, Ron. "The Children of God." TIME OUT, 182 (17-23 August 1973) 10-13.

1576. Kirk, Russel. "COG Widens the Gap." NATIONAL REVIEW, 16 March 1973. p. 314.

1577. Kittler, Glenn D. THE JESUS KIDS AND THEIR LEADERS. New York: Warner Paperback Library, 1972. pp. 138-47.

1578. Moore, Thomas. "Where Have All the Children of God Gone?" NEW TIMES, 4 October 1974. pp. 32-36, 38-41.

1579. Newman, Joseph, ed. THE RELIGIOUS REAWAKENING IN AMERICA.
       Washington, D.C.: U.S. News & World Report, 1972. pp. 33, 37-39, 127.

1580. Newsweek. "Children of Moses." NEWSWEEK, 28 October 1974. p. 70.

1581. ———. "Days in the Life of the Children of God." NEWSWEEK, 30 March
       1971. pp. 59-65.

1582. ———. "Defreaking Jesus Freaks." NEWSWEEK, 12 March 1973. p. 44.

1583. ———. "Generation Gap." NEWSWEEK, 22 November 1971. pp. 89-90.

1584. Omdal, S. CHILDREN OF GOD. England: Stavanger, 1974.

1585. Parmeter, B.W. "Letter to the Editor." TIME, 14 February 1972. p. 4.

1586. Time. "Children of Doom." TIME, 18 February 1974. p. 90.

1587. ———. "Following the Leader." TIME, 11 December 1978. p. 36.

1588. ———. "Open Season on Sects." TIME, 20 August 1972. p. 83.

1589. ———. "Tracking the Children of God—Will the Real Moses Please Come
       Down From the Mountain?" TIME, 22 August 1977. p. 48.

       Cites items 1677 and 1778, and in turn is cited in item 1645.

1590. ———. "Whose Children?" TIME, 24 January 1972. pp. 51, 53.

1591. U.S. News and World Report. "A Day in the Life of the Children of
       God." U.S. NEWS AND WORLD REPORT, 20 March 1972. p. 65.

1592. ———. "Religious Cults: Newest Magnet for Youth." U.S. NEWS AND
       WORLD REPORT, 80 (14 June 1976) 52-54.

1593. Wallis, Roy. "Moses David's Sexy God." NEW HUMANIST (U.K.), 93
       (May-August 1977) 12-14.

1594. ———. "Fishing for Men." THE HUMANIST, 38 (1978) 14-16.

1595. Warnock, Steve. "Child of God Flees From Doctors." SUNDAY
       (Australia), 25 March 1979. p. 7.

D. NEWSPAPER ARTICLES

Articles on the COG published in newspapers are also generally oriented toward informing the general public about the group. Like the journalistic articles in Section C, these too tend to be critical and to focus on the sensational aspects of the COG.

1596. Anderson, Godfrey. "Child of God Finds Commune Something Like Army." FORT WORTH STAR-TELEGRAM, 31 October 1971.

1597. ------. "'Children' Answer Parental Charge." FORT WORTH STAR TELEGRAM, 7 November 1971.

1598. Arnett, Peter. "Family Kidnaps Son From Sect." HOUSTON CHRONICLE, 24 November 1974. p. 2

1599. Carman, John. "Message Wins Battle for God's Mind." MINNEAPOLIS STAR, 11 December 1975. pp. A-1, 9.

1600. Chicago Sun-Times. "Sect Is Target of Parents Drive." CHICAGO SUN-TIMES, 22 February 1972. p. 17.

1601. Clyde, Velma. "Family Arrives in 'Prophet Bus' to Preach the Gospel." OREGONIAN (Portland), 29 January 1972.

1602. Cockburn, Alexander and James Ridgeway. "Cult Politics Comes of Age." THE VILLAGE VOICE, 23 (November 1978) 1, 13.

1603. Commercial Appeal. "Fundamentalists Put Importance on Comet." COMMERCIAL APPEAL (Memphis, TN), 29 December 1973. p. 14.

1604. Cotton, Crosbie. "Cult Member Dies Refusing Treatment." THE CALGARY HERALD, 17 March 1980. p. 1.

Continues story of item 1605.

1605. ------. "Dying City Mother Refuses Treatment, Awaits a Miracle." THE CALGARY HERALD, 14 March 1980. A-1-2.

Story continued in item 1604.

1606. ------. "They Are Right From the Pits of Hell." THE CALGARY HERALD, 26 March 1980. pp. B-1-2.

1607. ------. "Woman Wants to Save Her Sister From Cult." THE CALGARY HERALD, 18 March 1980. p. B-1.

Completes story of items 1604 and 1605.

1608.   Craig, Jim. "Salvation Found or a Prison." HOUSTON POST, 23 October
        1971. p. AA-14.

1609.   Dart, John. "Does Religious Commune Have Spell Over Youth?"
        MILWAUKEE JOURNAL, 18 October 1971. p. 1.

1610.   Detroit Free Press. "Mom Is Happy Her Son Joined Cult." DETROIT
        FREE PRESS, 6 November 1971.

1611.   Fenly, Leigh. "Daughter Refused Their Helping Hand." THE OAKLAND
        TRIBUNE, 6 June 1979. p. 18.

1612.   ------. "On Losing a Child to a Cult." THE OAKLAND TRIBUNE, 5 June
        1979. p. 22.

1613.   Fiske, Edward B. "Radical Group Leaving U.S." DENVER POST, 19
        August 1972. p. 8.

1614.   Fort Worth Star-Telegram. "Place at Thurber Not Very Typical: God
        Never Left Out of Learning Chores." FORT WORTH STAR-
        TELEGRAM, 15 August 1971. p. A-17.

1615.   Greene, D.S.A. "God's Hippie Children, Furious Parents Say Revivalists
        Are Possessed." NATIONAL OBSERVER, 15 April 1972. pp. 1, 16.

1616.   Griffis, Frank and Bob Stamp. "House Filled with Uncommon Youth."
        SUNDAY EAGLE (Bryan/College Station, TX), 25 July 1971.

1617.   Harris, Harvey. "'Kidnapped' Youth Was 'on a Trip with Jesus.'" DAILY
        NEWS (Greemsboro, NC), 28 August 1975. p. B-2.

1618.   Harvey, Duston. "'Children of God' Are Under Fire." INDEPENDENT
        JOURNAL, 31 December 1971. p. 15.

1619.   Houston Post. "Children of God Urges Members Go Home for Holidays."
        HOUSTON POST, 23 November 1971.

1620.   Israel, Mae. "Religious Sect Members Plead Guilty." DAILY NEWS
        (Greensboro, NC), 30 July 1975. B-1,2.

1621.   Journal-Tribune. "'Children of God' Using Sex to Recruit." JOURNAL-
        TIMES (Marysville, OH), 7 December 1979. p. 10.

1622.   Kinsolving, Lester. "The Children of God Stomp Up a Storm." SAN
        FRANCISCO SUNDAY EXAMINER AND CHRONICLE, 26 March 1972.
        p. B-6.

1623.   Las Vegas Sun. "Family's Love Pierces 'Cult' Barriers." LAS VEGAS
        SUN, 4 August 1975. p. 1.

1624.   Memminger, Charles. n.t. HONOLULU STAR BULLETIN, 6 October
        1980.

1625.   Milwaukee Journal. n.t. MILWAUKEE JOURNAL, 18 October 1971. pp.
        1,2.

1626. Mooney, William, William Clements and Lois Willie. "Capture to a Creed of Love and Doom." CHICAGO SUN TIMES DAILY NEWS, 5-6 April 1975. pp. 1, 10.

1627. ⸺. "Cult Firmly Believes 'Us Against World.'" CHICAGO SUN TIMES DAILY NEWS, 8 April 1975.

1628. ⸺. "Why Young People Become Religious Zealots." CHICAGO SUN TIMES DAILY NEWS, 7 April 1975. pp. 1, 10.

1629. National Catholic Register. "New York State Investigation Includes Claim Children of God Abused Members." NATIONAL CATHOLIC REGISTER, 1 December 1974. p. 2.

1630. National Star. "Not All God's Children Got Wings." NATIONAL STAR, 26 October 1974. p. 13.

1631. Olson, Lynne. "Free Choice for Youth? Parents vs. the Parents." CHICAGO SUN-TIMES, 24 June 1973. p. 2.

1632. Parmley, Helen. "Children of God: 'Other Side' Told." DALLAS MORNING NEWS, 17 October 1971. p. A-33.

1633. Redmont, Dennis. "Children of God Find Home Away From Home in Libya." THE WASHINGTON POST, 5 August 1977. B-14.

Corresponds to item 1635.

1634. ⸺. "'Children of God' Find Home in Libya." LOS ANGELES TIMES, 23 July 1977. p. I-25.

Corresponds to item 1634.

1635. Ruppert, R. "The Children of God." SEATTLE TIMES, 17 October 1971. pp. A-1, B-6, 10.

1636. Sanders, Bob-Ray. "Children of God, Backers Speak Out." FORT WORTH STAR TELEGRAM, 17 October 1971.

1637. ⸺. "This Is It ... Something I Could Give My Life To ... " FORT WORTH STAR-TELEGRAM, 15 August 1971. p. A-16.

1638. Seattle "Times." n.t., SEATTLE "TIMES," 13 March 1974. p. A-15.

1639. Spanek, Gerianne. "Ex-Cult Member Says She Was Told Not to Think." THE DAILY PRESS (Utica, NY), 2 June 1980. pp. 9, 16.

Story continued in item 1640.

1640. ⸺. "Ex-Cultist Unable to Make Decisions: Return to Society Difficult." THE DAILY PRESS (Utica, NY), 3 June 1980. pp. 6-7.

Continues story from item 1639.

1641. Stoner, Carroll. "The Making of Modern Cultists." BOSTON SUNDAY
       GLOBE, 26 November 1978. p. 1.

1642. Sunday People. n.t. SUNDAY PEOPLE, 24 September 1972. p. 4.

1643. Townsend, Anne. "What About Our Children." BRITISH WEEKLY, 3
       November 1978. p. 6.

1644. Vobejda, Barbara. n.t. HONOLULU ADVERTISER, 9 September 1980.

1645. The Washington Post. "'Mo Letter' Reportedly Asks Disbandment of
       Organization." THE WASHINGTON POST, 5 August 1977. p. B-14.

       Cites item 1589.

1646. Weber, Debbie. "Audrey 'Escaped' From Children of God." NATIONAL
       COURIER, 2 April 1975. pp. 12-13.

       Corresponds to items 1647 and 1648.

1647. ------. "Audrey's Experience with Children of God." THE TAMPA
       TRIBUNE, 7 February 1976. pp. 3-6.

       Corresponds to items 1646 and 1978.

1648. ------. "Defendents Fought Mind Control." NATIONAL COURIER, 9
       July 1976. p. 31.

       Corresponds to items 1646 and 1647.

1649. Wicker, Jim. "Four Members of Cult Face Charges in Court." Record
       (Greensboro, NC), 29 July 1975.

E. GOVERNMENT INVESTIGATIONS

A limited number of government documents concerning the COG have been produced. These have been reports from official investigations of the group's allegedly illegal activities and practices.

1650. Lefkowtiz, Louis J., Office of the Attorney General of the State of New York, INTERIM REPORT ON THE ACTIVITIES OF THE CHILDREN OF GOD, 8 January 1974, 65 pp.

Published in updated form as — REPORT ON THE ACTIVITIES OF THE CHILDREN OF GOD, 10 September 1974, 65 pp.

1651. State of California, Senate Select Committee on Children and Youth, HEARING ON THE IMPACT OF CULTS ON TODAY'S YOUTH, Held at California State University, Northridge, 24 August 1974.

1652. U.S. Senate, TRANSCRIPT OF PROCEEDINGS: INFORMATION MEETING ON THE CULT PHENOMENON IN THE UNITED STATES, Washington, D.C.: U.S. Senate, 5 February 1979, pp 64,76.

Made available in mimeographed form by: American Family Foundation; Maurice Davis; and Ted Patrik.

1653. Vermont Senate, Special Investigating Committee, n.t., Montpelier: Vermont Senate, 18 August 1976.

1654. Wallenstein, Herbert J. FINAL REPORT ON THE ACTIVITIES OF THE CHILDREN OF GOD, Submitted to Hon. L.J. Lefkowitz, Attorney General of the State of New York, Albany: Charity Frauds Bureau, 30 September 1974, 65 pp.

Supersedes item 1650.

F. ANTI-COG MATERIAL

No other group in the Jesus Movement has faced as much negative reaction and criticism as the COG. Much of this has been expressed in print, as books and as articles in magazines and journals.

A significant part of the polemical material on the COG has come from one organization—Free Our Sons and Daughters from the Children of God (FREECOG). Formed by parents in 1971, it was one of the first "anti-cult" groups to emerge. It claimed that the Children were victims of kidnapping, brainwashing, drug and hypnotic control, and extortion. Its answer to the COG was to rescue members from the group in order to unconvert them. By soliciting the help of Ted Patrick, the deprogramming movement was thus kicked off. The group was later renamed Citizens Freedom Foundation as it expanded its attention to other cult groups, but an emphasis upon the evils of the COG and the need for deprogramming remains.

Another major enemy of the COG has been the various Jesus People groups which have attacked the COG in their newspapers and magazines. They have generally sought to disassociate the COG from the rest of the Jesus Movement by criticizing its heretical beliefs and practices. In so doing, an effort is also made to "reach" members of the COG and/or to warn potential converts.

1655. Acts 17. INDEX TO COUNTERCULT RESOURCES. La Mesa, CA: Acts 17, 1978.

Superseded by item 1656.

1656. ——. WHERE TO TURN FOR HELP AGAINST THE CULTS. La Mesa, CA: Acts 17, 1981. 19 pp.

Supersedes item 1655.

1657. Alnor, William with David Clark. "Other Gospels, New Religions: Church of Bible Understanding." SPIRITUAL COUNTERFEITS PROJECT NEWSLETTER, 6 (May–June 1980) 5-7.

1658. American Family Foundation. "Children of God." FOUNDATION NEWS, 29 June 1979. p. 1.

1659. ——. "Children of God—Update." THE ADVISOR, 2 (April 1980) p. 3.

1660. ——. "Ex-Children of God Member Wins $1.5 Million." THE ADVISOR, 1 (October 1979) 1.

1661. ——. "New Religious Movements Up-Date." NEWS, 2 (September 1978) 59-60.

1662. American Jewish Congress, Commission on Law, Social Action and Urban Affairs. "The Cults and the Law." CLSA/UA REPORTS, 2 February 1978. p. 12.

1663. Anti-Defamation League of B'nai B'rith. "ADL Research Report: The Children of God." New York: Research Department, Civil Rights Division, Anti-Defamation League, March 1979. 10 pp.

1664. Bjornstad, James. "Taught to Hate Their Parents, 'Children of God' Flee Prosecution." Mimeographed. Oakland, NJ: Institute of Comtemporary Christianity, n.d.

1665. ------. "Where Have All the 'Children' (of God) Gone?" Mimeographed. Oakland, NJ: Institute of Contemporary Christianity, n.d.

1666. Branson, Ron, ed. "The Children of God: Their Bizarre Development." Alert Sheet #31. Mimeographed. North Hollywood: The Alert Sheet Publication Ministry, 1980. 4 pp.

Continues the story of item 1667.

1667. ------. "The Children of God: Their Blissful Debut." Alert Sheet #30. Mimeographed. North Hollywood: The Alert Sheet Publication Ministry, 1980. 4 pp.

Story continued in item 1666.

1668. Buzz. "The Children of God: A New Sect in the Making." Mimeographed. n.p., November 1973. 2 pp.

1669. Carruth, Joseph. "Other Gospels, New Religions: The Children of God (a.k.a. Family of Love)." SPIRITUAL COUNTERFEITS PROJECT NEWSLETTER, 6 (July-September 1980) 4-6.

1670. Christian Information Network. CULTS. Pine Lake, GA: Christian Information Network, 1981.

1671. The Christian Research Institute. "'The Children of God.' Fact Sheet." Mimeographed. Juan Capistrano, CA: The Christian Research Institute, n.d. 3 pp.

1672. Citizens Freedom Foundation—Information Services. "Did Cult Abduct Two Children? 'Defector' Blames Spouse, 10 Others." NEWS, 5 (1 October 1980) 2.

Story continued in item 1673.

1673. ------. "Mother Accuses Cult Members." NEWS, 5 (1 December 1980) 3.

Continues the story of item 1672.

1674. ------. "News Briefs." NEWS, 5 (4 February 1980) 8.

1675. David C. Cook Publishing Company. DISTINCTIVES - STUDY 5. Elgin, IL: David C. Cook, 1980.

1676.   Copp, Cornelius. "The Children of God: Response to Report of the New York Attorney General." Mimeographed. Dallas: The Author, 1974. 20 pp.

1677.   Cornerstone. "God Bless You—And: Good Bye! By Moses David." CORNERSTONE, 6 (July 1977) 9.

Commented upon in item 1678.

1678.   ——. "Goodbye." CORNERSTONE, 6 (July 1977) 9-10.

Comments upon item 1677.

1679.   ——. "Moses & His Children." CORNERSTONE, 29 (1979) 11 pp.

Reprinted as Jesus People USA-FGM. "Moses & His Children." Mimeographed. Chicago: JPUSA Productions, 1979. 6 pp.

1680.   Dayspring Publications. "Children of God." DAYSPRING, 1 (June 1978) 1-8.

1681.   Deo Gloria Outreach. n.t. NEWS & VIEWS, 2 (March 1980) 1.

1682.   Ehrenborg, Todd. "The Children Of God." Mimeographed. San Juan Capistrano, CA: Christian Research Institute, n.d. 19 pp.

1683.   False Prophets Project. WHO ARE THE CHILDREN OF GOD? Heidebeck, Heerde, Holland: Dilaram Houses, 1976. 23 pp.

1684.   Frampton, K.P. "Beware—'The Children of God.'" Mimeographed. Bromley, Kent, England: K.P. Frampton, 1972. 16 pp.

1685.   ——. "The 'Children of God' Movement." Mimeographed. Bromley, Kent, England: Deo Gloria Press, 1973. 12 pp.

1686.   FREECOG. BEWARE OF THE CHILDREN OF GOD. Guelph, Ontario: FREECOG, n.d. 48 pp.

1687.   Hansen, Kathy. "Ex-COG." Mimeographed. Minneapolis: The Author, November 1980. 2 pp.

1688.   ——. "Ex-COG." CITIZENS FREEDOM FOUNDATION—NEWS, 6 (July 1981) 2.

1689.   ——. "Letter From Ex-Children of God." CITIZENS FREEDOM FOUNDATION—NEWS, 1 January 1981. p. 6.

1690.   Herrin, John W. "Why We Should Pray for the Children of God." Mimeographed. Chicago: Jesus People U.S.A., 1974. 2 pp.

1691.   Hopkins, Joseph M. "Children of God—Update." THE ADVISOR, 2 (April 1980) 42-45.

1692.   ——. "Chronological Chart of David Berg's and the Children of God's History." SPIRITUAL COUNTERFEITS PROJECT NEWSLETTER, 6 (July-September 1980) 9.

1693.   ——. "A Comparison of Teachings." SPIRITUAL COUNTERFEITS
        PROJECT NEWSLETTER, 6 (July-September 1980) 7-9.

1694.   ——. "The Way, the Plain Truth, Moon and 'Mo': Keeping Up With the
        New Cults." CITIZENS FREEDOM FOUNDATION NEWS, 5 (1 June
        1980) 5.

1695.   Hultquist, Lee. THEY FOLLOWED THE PIPER. Plainfield, NJ: Logos
        International, 1977.

1696.   Institute of Contemporary Christianity. WHO ARE THE CHILDREN OF
        GOD? Oakland, NJ: Institute Of Contemporary Christianity, 1979. 58
        pp.

1697.   Jesus People USA. "Why We Should Pray for the Children of God."
        Mimeographed. Chicago: Jesus People USA, n.d. 2 pp.

1698.   Knoblock, James. "The Children of David: A Biblical Examination of
        Moses David and the Children of God." Mimeographed. Escondido, CA,
        1977.

1699.   Lochhaas, Philip H. HOW TO RESPOND TO THE NEW CHRISTIAN
        RELIGIONS. St. Louis: Concordia, 1979. pp. 18-19.

1700.   McManus, Una and John Charles Cooper. NOT FOR A MILLION
        DOLLARS. Nashville: Impact Books, 1980.

1701.   MacPherson, Shirley. "Report on the American Cult Known as 'the
        Children of God.'" Mimeographed. n.p., 1972. 14 pp.

1702.   Martin, Walter, ed. with Gretchen Passantino. "The Children Of God
        (The Family Of Love)." THE NEW CULTS. Santa Ana, CA: Vision House,
        1978. pp. 143-201.

1703.   Moriconi, John. CHILDREN OF GOD, FAMILY OF LOVE. Downers
        Grove, IL: InterVarsity Press, 1980. 39 pp.

1704.   Outreach for Jesus. "Why We Should Pray for the Children of God."
        Mimeographed. London: Outreach For Jesus, n.d. 4 pp.

1705.   Patrik, Ted with Tom Dulack. LET OUR CHILDREN GO! New York:
        E.P. Dutton, 1976.

1706.   Peterson, William J. "The Children of God and the Jesus Movement."
        THOSE CURIOUS NEW CULTS. New Cannaan, CT: Keats, 1975. pp.
        121-36.

1707.   Philpott, Kent. "Open Letter." HOLLYWOOD FREE PRESS, 3 (1971).

1708.   Rudin, A. James and Marcia R. Rudin. PRISON OR PARADISE? THE
        NEW RELIGIOUS CULTS. Philadelphia: Fortress Press, 1980. pp. 7, 13,
        24, 25, 74-82, 99-1-1, 122, 139.

1709. Sparks, Jack. "The Children of God." THE MINDBENDERS: A LOOK AT CURRENT CULTS. Nashville: Thomas Nelson, 1977. pp. 155-83.

1710. Spiritual Counterfeits Project. "The Children of God." RE-5. Mimeographed. Berkeley: Spirutual Counterfeits Project, 1974. 1 p.

1711. ———. "Children of God." SPIRITUAL COUNTERFEITS PROJECT NEWSLETTER, 2 (January 1976) 2.

1712. Stoner, Carroll and Jo Anne Parke. ALL GODS CHILDREN: THE CULT EXPERIENCE—SALVATION OR SLAVERY? Radnor, PA: Chilton, 1977. pp. 10, 19-23, 48-51, 64-67.

1713. Tapla, Norma Iris. "Peculiar Religious Cult Budding In Puerto Rico— Brainwashing or Genuine Devotion?" CITIZEN'S FREEDOM FOUNDATION—INFORMATIONAL SERVICES, 5 (7 March 1980) 4-5.

1714. Wasson, Jack. "Children of God." Mimeographed. Dallas: Easy Yoke Ministries, 1975. 9 pp.

1715. Wasson, Jack and Connie Wasson. "Keeping Up with Mo." CORNERSTONE, 6 (June-July 1977) 13.

G. AUDIO MATERIAL

The audio material on the COG is in the same critical vein as the anti-COG printed material. The audio items, however, tend to give a more systematic description of the group in the process. There is also a stronger emphasis upon refuting COG theology and practices from a Biblical perspective, and often advice is given on how to witness to members, relate to ex-members, etc.

1716. Chiara, John. THE CHILDREN OF GOD SEX CULT. Covina, CA: Cult Exodus for Christ, n.d. Cassette tape.

1717. Deo Gloria Promotions. CULT EXPLOSION. Bromley, Kent, England: Deo Gloria Promitions, n.d. Film.

1718. Enroth, Ronald. COUNTERING THE CULTS. Oakland, NJ: Institute of Contemporary Christianity, 1980. Cassette tape #4.

1719. ------. MYSTERY, MYSTICISM AND MIND CONTROL. Oakland, NJ: Institute of Contemporary Christianity, 1980. Cassette tape #3.

1720. ------. NEW AGE CULTS: FALSE RELIGION IN CONTEMPORARY GARB. Oakland, NJ: Institute of Contemporary Christianity, 1980. Cassette tape #1.

1721. ------. THE PRACTICES OF THE CULTS. Oakland, NJ: Institute of Contemporary Christianity, 1980. Cassette tape #2.

1722. Martin, Walter. THE CHILDREN OF GOD? San Juan Capistrano, CA: Christian Research Institute, n.d. Cassette tape.

1723. Passantino, Gretchen. THE CHILDREN OF GOD. Santa Ana, CA: Christian Apologetics: Research and Information Service, Spring 1981. Cassette tape.

1724. Street, R. Alan. CHILDREN OF GOD (FAMILY OF LOVE). Finksburg, MD: Street Meetings, Inc., n.d. Cassette tape #CE-21A.

1725. Wasson, Jack and Connie Wasson. CASSETTE TAPE OF THEIR STORY IN THE COG. Berkeley: New Religious Movements Library, Graduate Theological Union, n.d. Cassette tape.

APPENDIX

LOCATIONS OF COLLECTED COG MATERIAL

1726. The Institute for the Study of American Religion, Box 1311, Evanston, Illinois 60201. (312) 271-3419. Dr. J. Gordon Melton, Director.

1727. Practical Apologetics and Christian Evangelism (P.A.C.E.), P.O. Box 1901, Orange, California 92668. Kurt Van Gordon, Director.

1728. Program for the Study of New Religious Movements in America, 2451 Ridge Road, Berkeley, California 94709. (415) 841-2828. Dr. Jacob Needleman, Director; Diane Choquette, Librarian.

AUTHOR INDEX

Acts 17. Items 1655 and 1656.

Alexander, Shana. Item 1567.

The Alliance for the Preservation of Religious Liberty. Item 1568.

Alnor, William with David Clark. Item 1657.

American Family Foundation. Items 1658 through 1661.

American Jewish Congress. Item 1662.

Americans Preserving Religious Liberty. Item 1569.

Anderson, Godfrey. Items 1596 and 1597.

Anthony, Dick and Thomas Robbins. Item 1418.

Anti-Defamation League. Item 1663.

Apollos and David Berg (Moses David). Item 1021.

Arnett, Peter. Item 1598.

The Baptist Messenger. Item 1482.

Barker, Eileen. Items 1419 and 1483.

Beckford, James A. Item 1420.

Berg, David (Moses David). Items 1 through 966, 968 through 1019, 1054 through 1056, 1060 through 1071, 1100 through 1104, 1120 through 1121, 1157 through 1226, and 1230 through 1339.

Berg David (Moses David) and Eve Berg (Mother Eve). Item 1122.

Berg, David (Moses David) and Joel Wordsworth. Item 1072.

Berg, David (Moses David) and Maria. Item 967.

Berg, Debra, Mother Eve David, Faith David and the Mo Education Classes. Item 1020.

Berg, Eve (Mother Eve David). Items 1022 through 1031.

Berg, Virginia Brandt (Grandmother). Items 1032 through 1035, 1073, 1105 through 1106, and 1340 through 1362.

Bjornstad, James. Items 1664 and 1665.

Bourgoin, Mary Fay. Item 1570.

Branson, Ron. Items 1666 and 1667.

Brown, Marvin. Items 1421 and 1422.

Bruning, Fred, Anthony Collings and Carolyn Paul. Items 1571.

Buzz. Item 1668.

Campus Ministry Communications. Item 1484.

Carlos. Item 1036.

Carman, John. Item 1599.

Carroll, Jackson W. Item 1423.

Carruth, Joseph. Item 1669.

Cartoon, Jacob. Item 1057.

Cephas. Item 1074.

Challenge. Items 1485 through 1487.

Chiara, John. Item 1716.

Chicago Sun-Times. Item 1600.

The Children of God. Items 1058, 1075 through 1094, 1107 through 1118, 1123 through 1148, 1150 through 1156, 1229, and 1363 through 1417.

Christ for the Nations. Item 1488.

Christian Information Network. Item 1670.

Christian Inquirer. Item 1489.

Christian Research Institute. Item 1671.

Citizens Freedom Foundation. Items 1672 through 1674.

Christianity Today. Items 1490 through 1497.

Clyde, Velma. Item 1601.

Cockburn, Alexander and James Ridgeway. Item 1602.

Cohen, Daniel. Item 1424.

Hefley, James C. Item 1518.

Henderson, C. William. Item 1444.

Herrin, John W. Item 1690.

Hollenweger, Walter J. Item 1519.

Hopkins, Joseph M. Items 1520 through 1525, and 1691 through 1694.

Houston Post. Item 1619.

Hudson, Winthrop S. Item 1445.

Hulstquist, Lee. Item 1695.

Hunt, Dave. Item 1526.

Hyde, Margaret O. Item 1446.

Inkletter, Hart. Item 1059.

Institute of Contemporary Christianity. Item 1696.

Israel, Mae. Item 1620.

Jacob, Michael. Item 1527.

Jesus People U.S.A. Item 1697.

Jorstad, Erling. Item 1528.

Journal-Tribune. Item 1621.

Kelly, Dean M. Item 1529.

Kinsolving, Lester. Item 1622.

Kirk, Russel. Item 1576.

Kirschner Associates, Inc. and the Institute for the Study of American Religion. Item 1447.

Kittler, Glenn D. Item 1577.

Knight, Walter L. Item 1530.

Knoblock, James. Item 1698.

Langford, Harris. Item 1531.

Larsen, David L. Item 1532.

Las Vegas Sun. Item 1623.